ALSO BY MARVIN HARRIS

Culture, People, Nature:
  An Introduction to General Anthropology, Third Edition

Cultural Materialism:
  The Struggle for a Science of Culture

Cannibals and Kings:
  The Origins of Cultures

Cows, Pigs, Wars and Witches:
  The Riddles of Culture

The Rise of Anthropological Theory

Patterns of Race in the Americas

The Nature of Cultural Things

Town and Country in Brazil

America
Now

THE
ANTHROPOLOGY
OF A CHANGING
CULTURE

Marvin Harris

A TOUCHSTONE BOOK
Published by Simon and Schuster
NEW YORK

For Madeline Harris

A Touchstone Book

Published by Simon & Schuster, Inc.
Simon & Schuster Building
Rockefeller Center
1230 Avenue of the Americas
New York, New York 10020

TOUCHSTONE and colophon are registered trademarks of Simon & Schuster, Inc.

Designed by Eve Kirch

Manufactured in the United States of America

10 9 8 7 6 5 4 3 2 1
10 9 8 7   Pbk.

Library of Congress Cataloging in Publication Data

Harris, Marvin. date.
   America now.

   Bibliography: p.
   Includes index.
   1. United States—Social conditions—1970—
I. Title.
HN59.H27 1981 973.92   81-9132
                          AACR2

ISBN 0-671-43148-X
ISBN 0-671-45701-2 Pbk.

Contents

1

Introduction

This book is about cults, crime, shoddy goods, and the shrinking dollar. It's about porno parlors, and sex shops, and men kissing in the streets. It's about daughters shacking up, women on the rampage, marriages postponed, divorces on the rise, and no one having kids. It's about old ladies getting mugged and raped, people shoved in front of trains, and shoot-outs at gas pumps. And letters that take weeks to get delivered, waiters who throw the food at you, rude sales help, and computers that bill you for things you never bought. It's about broken benches, waterless fountains, cracked windows, dirty toilets, crater-filled roads, graffiti-covered buildings, slashed paintings, toppled statues, stolen books. It's about shoelaces that break in a week, bulbs that keep burning out, pens that won't write, cars that rust, stamps that don't stick, stitches that don't hold, buttons that pop off, zippers that jam, planes that lose their engines, reactors that leak, dams that burst, roofs that collapse. . . . It's about astrologers, shamans, exorcists, witches, and angels in space suits. . . . It's about a lot of other things that are new and strange in America today.

Violent crime is at an all-time high. Children are disrespectful. Vandalism is rampant. Premarital and extramarital sex for both men and women have become the norm; the birthrate is at an all-time low. There are more divorces and broken families than ever before, and there is a sharp rise in the number of homosexuals or at least in the number of people who publicly express and advertise homosexual preferences. There has also been a proliferation of California-style cults, a great burgeoning of interest in shamanism, astrology, witchcraft, exorcism, fundamentalism, and mind-changing sects ranging from est to the "Moonies" and Jim Jones's jungle temple. At the same time people have lost pride in their work. Sales help are uncooperative and ill-informed. It's hard to find competent secretaries, waiters and waitresses, bank clerks, and telephone operators. Also, America has lost its reputation for producing high-quality industrial goods. Automobiles and appliances are in constant need of repair and many items break as soon as their warranties expire. The whole economy seems to have gone berserk. A bizarre kind of inflation has attacked the dollar. Prices keep rising even though consumer demand slumps and unemployment gets worse. Billions doled to people on welfare get spent on shoes and clothing made in Taiwan or Korea while American shoe, clothing, and textile factories go out of business.

Is there a relationship between inflation and the increase in self-identified homosexuals? Between rising divorce rates and shoddy consumer products? Between women's liberation and rising urban crime rates? Between the proliferation of far-out cults and the increase in rude and uncooperative sales help? Why is all this happening at the same time?

I have been studying peoples and cultures other than my own—in South America, India, and Africa—for over three decades. In the back of my mind I always thought that the study of customs and institutions in remote areas of the world might someday be useful for understanding my native land. Can insights gleaned from research in other societies now contribute to an explanation of why American customs and institutions have changed so radically?

One important point that anthropologists have always made is that aspects of social life which do not seem to be related to each other, actually are related. When one part of a culture changes, it has an effect on other parts that may not be seen at once. Often, the connection between one part and another may not be perceived by the very people whose lives are most affected by what is happening. If this is true, then we cannot hope to understand why any particular aspect of a people's way of life has changed if we view it in isolation and do not study the interconnectedness of all the changes taking place —or at least, the interconnectedness of all the major changes.

Trained to live alone among strangers and to record and explain the diversity of human customs and institutions, anthropologists acquire a view of culture that is broader—more "holistic"—than that of other social scientists. As lone field-workers, preceded only by missionaries or occasional traders, anthropologists have had to cope with the problem of describing whole cultures and of seeing how the various parts of whole cultures fit together.

Bronislav Malinowski's classic studies of the Trobriand Islanders typify the anthropological "imagination." Malinowski tried to study everything: how the Trobrianders plant their gardens, sail their canoes, placate their ancestors, steal crops by means of magical incantations, find wives and husbands, and position themselves for sexual intercourse. He described their family life, their political organization, their system of chiefs and headmen, as well as the meanings they give to life and death. Of course, even a Malinowski could not really succeed in studying everything. Human social life in the smallest primitive bands and villages is far too rich and complicated to be grasped in its entirety. But like many other anthropologists he did try to draw a sketch of customs and institutions embracing the subject matter ordinarily studied by experts in several different disciplines such as economics, sociology, political science, psychology, geography, and history. I feel that something like this broad perspective is needed to understand changes in customs and institutions in complex nations just as much as it is needed to understand small primitive societies.

In the holistic tradition of anthropology, this book provides a general framework for understanding the bewildering changes taking place in America today. Since America is immensely more populous and complicated than a Trobriand village or the small town I myself once studied in the backlands of Brazil, this may seem to be a vain and foolish endeavor. But there are mitigating circumstances. In some respects it may actually be easier to gain a holistic view of American culture than of small exotic villages or tribes. One does not have to consume months painfully acquiring the rudiments of a new language, nor need one work alone groping toward an elementary grasp of utterly new customs and institutions. Here the problem is not that an anthropologist has to act as a proxy economist, sociologist, psychologist, and the rest. All the specialists have already been here, launched thousands of research projects, interviewed millions of native "informants," and written enough articles and books to fill the Grand Canyon. Here it is the anthropologist who arrives last on the scene and has to contend not with a dearth of information but with a surfeit of information.

In other words, the problem of making sense out of the changes taking place in America today may be more a matter of having some general framework for showing the interconnectedness of data in many different disciplines than it is a matter of being an expert in any one of those disciplines. But what kind of general framework shall we use?

Moral and spiritual values provide one kind of framework. Countless books and articles maintain that Americans have lost their forefathers' work ethic and puritan sense of discipline. In former years Americans worked and saved up for their pleasures. Now young people say they owe it to themselves to have a good time, to get everything that is coming to them—booze, drugs, food, travel, multiple orgasms—right away with no down payment and with no personal entanglements, marriage, or children to worry about. A variation on the same theme characterizes the new American culture as libertarian, open, permissive—a culture in which, as in ancient Rome, anything goes.

These are apt characterizations even though one can readily point to exceptions: the grim earnestness of today's college students competing for careers in medicine, law, engineering, and business administration, or the public-spirited environmentalist and conservationist movements. But let us suppose that, on balance, it is correct to say that a new sensualist, hedonistic, and narcissistic mood has overwhelmed the traditional American sense of duty, hard work, and self-discipline. Have we really gotten closer to understanding why America changed? I don't think so. We still have to answer the question of why traditional moral and spiritual values have lost their appeal.

Rather than start from the "top" of a culture—from changes in its moral and spiritual values—I have found that it is usually more enlightening to start from the "bottom"—that is, from changes in the way people conduct the practical and mundane affairs of their everyday lives. As an anthropologist, I am impressed most by the fact that in the new U.S.A., for example, people no longer earn their living the way they did a short while ago. The majority of Americans now produce services and information rather than goods. Not only do more people now work in offices, stores, and consulting rooms than in factories, but what they do at their jobs has also changed drastically because of automation and unionization. Also, looking back over the last fifty years I see that the whole sexual composition of the labor force has changed. Married women who formerly worked exclusively in the home now work outside the home almost as often as married men do. And the organizations for which people work are very different from what they used to be. Firms are much larger and more bureaucratic, and a surprising number of Americans now work for government rather than for private companies.

I think that this set of changes may provide the best framework for understanding how the pieces of American culture now fit together. Anthropologists have long known that when people change their way of making a living, unintended consequences are likely to be felt in a broad range of customs and institutions. For example, when primitive peoples turned from a life based on hunting to one based on planting crops and raising cattle, their family, government, and religion underwent a complete transformation. Hunters generally live in small migratory bands, lack property, are highly democratic, and tend to be monogamous. Agricultural peoples generally live in larger and more permanent settlements; accumulate property in land, houses, and furnishings; have powerful chiefs; and often take plural wives. In addition, as everyone knows, extensive cultural changes were brought about by advances in agriculture and by the introduction of the factory system and mass production. It seems worthwhile, therefore, to explore the possibility that changes in the quality of American goods and services, inflation, family life, sex, crime, welfare, and religion have something to do with the changes in the organization and type of work and the sexual composition of the U.S. labor force.

Obviously, the shift in the nature of work and in the organization and composition of the workforce cannot account for every detail of America's new life-styles. There is no single chain of causes and effects that can be followed out link by link from one basic change to all the others. Social change takes place more like the building of a web than the building of a chain. Many different causal strands cross and recross to form intricate designs in which each element has an independent role to play to some extent. But this does not mean that all of the strands are of equal size or carry equal weight; nor does it mean that the web has no center or that it lacks an overall structure. The purpose of this book is not to explain everything down to the latest sexual kink, tight-pants fad, or mugging technique. Rather, it is to determine if apparently unrelated trends in disparate aspects of the American way of life actually constitute an unintended but coherent process of change. By using a framework which emphasizes the central role of factors such as the participation of women in the labor force, automation, and the growing bureaucratic concentration of government and private enterprise, I do not think that I will be able to explain everything about U.S. culture. I merely hope that we shall find it possible to understand more about what is happening than if we simply were to blame everything on a spontaneous collapse of traditional moral and spiritual values.

Moreover, everything presented here must be regarded as tentative and approximate, not as final and beyond improvement. I do not claim to be in possession of the one and only ultimate truth about why America changed. The principles which have shaped this inquiry do not lead to the kinds of certainties that people seek through revelation or religious faith. I will be satisfied if I succeed in showing that there are plausible, rational, and connected explanations for features of American life that are commonly regarded as random, unintelligible, and disconnected, or as the handiwork of God or the devil.

This seems to me to be an important point to make since the belief that culture and history are beyond rational human comprehension is gaining strength. From all sides, obscurantists, romantics, and mystics have sought to discredit the idea that the solution to America's practical and spiritual problems can be attained through rational endeavor guided by objective analysis. Attacks against reason and objectivity are once again intellectually fashionable. Under the banner of what Berkeley philosopher Paul Feyerabend calls "epistemological anarchy," scholars denounce the pursuit of objective truth as a waste of time. The word is out that rival "paradigms" are merely "ships that pass in the night," and that the truths of reasoned inquiry are no different from the truths of intuition and drug-induced fantasies.

Scores of sociologists proclaim that valid knowledge of society consists exclusively of "insiders' " meanings and intentions, and that there can never be an objective account of what really happens when humans interact: "Truths are always for and within a community," they say.

Meanwhile, inspired by Carlos Castaneda's story of his apprenticeship to a fictional Yaqui Indian sorcerer, many of my colleagues have been extolling the advantages of "alternate nonwestern realities" and "the shamanic state of consciousness" in which one can turn into a coyote, see hundred-foot gnats, and enter the nether world through a hole in a tree trunk.

The belief among social scientists that the description of social life "has to be a fiction, a constitution of reality" has also been endorsed enthusiastically in literary circles. Almost everyone by now has heard the critic Ronald Sukenick's: "All versions of reality are in the nature of fiction. There's your story and my story, there's the journalist's story and the historian's story, there's the philosopher's story and the scientist's story. . . . reality is imagined."

In some circles, the attack against reason and objectivity is fast reaching the proportions of a crusade. Americans in unprecedented numbers are heeding the call of home-grown ayatollahs and born-again evangelists. As one convert to a fast-growing born-again TV church told *Washington Post* columnist Dick Dabney: "I believe in Jesus. Reason sucks. And that's everything I know."

What makes this great upswelling of obscurantist and irrational fervor so alarming is its close connection with visions of the end of Western civilization, and even of life on earth. Many millions of Americans have been dismayed and frustrated by the destruction of cherished institutions and values, ground down by taxes, bureaucratic inefficiency, unemployment, crime, and inflation until they no longer seem to care whether the world goes on or not. With A.D. 2000, the end of the second millennium looming a few short years ahead, could not the premonition of a cosmic Armageddon become a self-fulfilling prophecy? Already there are suggestions that the end is near and that there is nothing we can do about it. "It's all going up," said the born-again convert who thinks "reason sucks." "It's too late for anything."

Personally, I keep enough sleeping pills around the house to kill my wife and children in case of bad radiation burns.

These dark premonitions may be generated more by a lack of understanding of America's cultural predicament than by religious faith. Why hasn't the American dream come true? Why have so many things gone wrong? Lacking an objective understanding of social life, people imagine themselves in the grip of uncontrolled Satanic forces. But we, ordinary men and women, are the sole authors of our discontents. Seeking a better world, step by step, together, we have spun the web that holds us from our dreams. Trembling, we expect the embrace of an inhuman beast, but we are only waiting for ourselves.

The task of this book is to reassert the primacy of rational endeavor and objective knowledge in the struggle to save and renew the American dream. I disagree with those who say that all knowledge and action (or as Marxists put it, all "theory and practice") are "always for and within" a particular community, ethnic group, class, race, tribe, or sex. Anthropologists regard it as their solemn duty to represent the hopes and fears, values and goals, beliefs and rituals of different groups and communities seen from within, the way people who belong to these groups and communities perceive them to be, and the way they want them to be seen by others. But that can be only half the job. The other half is to describe and explain what people are actually saying and doing from the standpoint of the objective study of culture and history.

America urgently needs to reaffirm the principle that it is possible to carry out an analysis of social life which rational human beings will recognize as being true, regardless of whether they happen to be women or men, whites or blacks, straights or gays, employers or employees, Jews or born-again Christians. The alternative is to stand by helplessly as special interest groups tear the United States apart in the name of their "separate realities," or to wait until one of them grows strong enough to force its own irrational and subjective brand of reality on all the rest.

Let the reader be forewarned. This book does not contain a detailed set of prescriptions as to how America can regain its momentum toward affluence, democracy, and justice. This is not a "how to do it" book; it is a "why" book. I have no utopian claims to make nor can I propose any simple course of action. Yet is not the struggle to understand a problem part of its solution? If we cannot achieve a better understanding of social life, can we expect to change social life for the better? I have opinions and preferences, and I shall venture to say what they are. If my "whys" are correct, it should be possible to distinguish between desired outcomes that are plausible and those that are implausible, and I shall have something to say on that subject also.

But the central purpose of this work is to explain rather than to prescribe. I hope it will appeal to those who believe that the reasoned search for an objective understanding of nature and culture remains the most precious heritage of Western civilization.

2

Why Nothing Works

Is America "dying of a broken part"? When bolts supporting Hartford's Civic Center snapped, the entire steel-and-concrete roof plunged into the ten-thousand-seat auditorium. Luckily, the spectators had left a few hours earlier and no one was hurt. But one hundred and eleven people died when two aerial walkways in Kansas City's new Hyatt Regency Hotel crashed to the lobby floor. At Three Mile Island a relief valve got stuck in the open position and brought the nuclear core to the brink of a meltdown. A few months later a forty-five-cent circuit board in the military computer alert system signaled that the Soviet Union had just launched a missile attack. And in New York City, Los Angeles, Houston, Atlanta, and other cities, twenty-five hundred brand-new Grumman buses costing $130,000 each developed cracks and sagging rear ends as soon as they hit their first pothole and had to be removed from service. Commenting on the flaws in the vehicle's design, Alan Kiepper, general manager of the Atlanta Transit Authority, quipped: "This was a horse, designed by a committee, which came out a dromedary."

In the aborted operation intended to rescue the American hostages from Teheran, three of the mission's eight helicopters broke down in the Iranian Desert. A crack in the sixteen-foot tail rotor blade disabled one, a broken fitting on a hydraulic pipe disabled another, and a malfunctioning gyroscope finished off the third. Apprised of what had gone wrong on the rescue mission, the owner of a household appliance repair shop in Brooklyn told reporter Michael Daly: "What do you expect? The United States can't even produce a good toaster anymore." The shop owner, Norma Treadwell, added, "Now nothing works."

America has become a land plagued by loose wires, missing screws, things that don't fit, things that don't last, things that don't work. Push the handle on the pop-up toaster and it won't stay down. Or it stays down and burns the toast. Newer models, says Treadwell, have short-lived thermostats instead of durable timers. Faulty thermostats also plague hair dryers and coffeemakers. Electric fans used to work forever; now the plastic blades develop cracks and have to be replaced. Vacuum cleaners have plastic handles that wobble and break; their cords come loose from the switch; their motors burn out. Tug hard on your shoelaces when they're a month old and they'll come apart. Or the little plastic tips come off and you can't pass the frayed ends through the holes. Go to the medicine chest for a bandaid. "Tear off end, pull string down," it says. But the string slips to the side and comes out. On the same principle, there is the packing bag for books. "Pull tab down." But the tab breaks off sending a shower of dirty fluff over the floor.

Louis Harris conducted a poll in 1979 in which 57 percent of the respondents said they were "deeply worried" about the poor quality of the products they were buying. Seventy-seven percent expressed the feeling that "manufacturers don't care about me." Based on a separate sampling of national opinion, *U.S. News & World Report* concluded "dissatisfaction runs wider and deeper than many experts suspected." Of the people responding to the pollsters' questions, 59 percent said they had returned one or more unsatisfactory products to the place of purchase during the preceding twelve months. A year later the figure had risen to 70 percent. According to a study published in the *Harvard Business Review,* 20 percent of all product purchases on the average lead to some form of dissatisfaction (other than price) among the purchasers.

Autos are high on the list of products that cause problems for their owners. About 30 percent of respondents reported they were dissatisfied or had a nonprice complaint about their cars. More than half of all complaints about auto repairs come from owners of vehicles still under new car warranties.

With the passage of federal highway safety and environmental protection legislation, huge recalls of vehicles with actually or potentially hazardous defects throw some light on the magnitude of the quality problems plaguing the U.S. auto industry. In 1979 for example, the Ford Motor Company recalled 16,000 of its 1979 Mustangs and Capris for defective power steering; 3,400 of its 1979 Mustangs for unsafe engine fans; 77,700 of its vans for defective front brake hoses; 400,000 Capris for front seat backs that could collapse and gear shift levers that could come apart; 70,000 of its light trucks for defects in wheel assemblies; and 390,000 of its 1969–1973 full-sized Fords, Mercurys, Meteors, and Lincoln Continentals for possible defects in the steering system. Meanwhile General Motors was recalling 172,000 of its 1977 and 1978 Monzas, Sunbirds, and Starfires for steering problems; 430,000 of its 1978 Pontiacs for defective pollution control devices; 372,000 of its 1977 and 1978 Cadillacs for possibly defective accelerator pedals; 19,500 cars of various models equipped with defective cruise control switches; 13,000 subcompacts for carburetor fuel-feed hose defects; 1,800,000 of its 1978 intermediate-sized cars and pickup trucks for defective front wheel-bearing assemblies; 41,500 Cadillac Sevilles equipped with electronic fuel injection engines that could cause fires; 1,300,000 full-size cars for front seat belts that can come loose under stress; and 16,000 of its 1979 light trucks for defective bolts in the steering arms.

But safety recall statistics alone will never properly memorialize the overall product-quality disaster embodied in America's aging fleet of gas-guzzling cars. Beyond being dangerous, they were massively inconvenient and unreliable. Fresh from the factory, windows and trunks leaked, bodies rattled, radiators boiled over, tires went flat. They were too heavy to be steered without power steering or to be stopped without power brakes. Their doors were too big to open next to other parked cars. Their curved side windows lacked once standard small triangular deflectors that in times gone by had served to cross-ventilate the front seat. Without these deflectors there was no way to get the airstream to enter the passenger compartment even while traveling at high speed with windows completely rolled down. "Fresh air" ducts merely supplied the passengers with air raised to engine temperature. Without air conditioning, many models became unusable even on relatively cool days. Because the interior dimensions had grown so huge, the driver could no longer reach across to close or open the window on the passenger side. This called for electric windows with motors housed inside the doors. The constant opening and slamming of the driver's door loosened the electric connections and the driver's window soon functioned intermittently. To pay tolls the driver then had to open the door and get out. When it rained, the driver got soaked, for while the car's shape kept out cooling breezes, its outward flaring body actually placed the top of the driver's head in a vertical line that was several inches beyond the roof. Windshield wipers were tucked into recessed compartments which collected leaves and trash and which froze solid after the first snowstorm. The thin wires sandwiched inside the windshield which replaced external antennas rendered the radio useless except for the closest and most powerful stations. Because the windshield had grown so huge, there was no place to put the rearview mirror. Gluing it to the windshield was a brilliant if temporary solution which ended when the surprised owner would open the door one morning and find the mirror staring at the roof from the middle of the front seat.

The U.S. auto industry serves as a convenient example of America's product-quality problems because so much of the public's economic well-being and safety depends on automobile-related jobs and on passenger car transportation. But quality disasters similar to that of the gas guzzlers characterize many different kinds of goods recently made in the U.S.A., even though their impact may be less dramatic. Hi fi records, for example. According to record store owners interviewed for the *Wall Street Journal,* the defect rate in major releases runs as high as 20 percent. Warped discs which cause needles to skip, scratchiness, pops, ticks, and other noises are the most frequent source of complaint.

What caused such an outpouring of defective and shoddy products? The problem cannot be that the United States literally doesn't know how to make a good toaster anymore. A nation capable of putting a whole computer on a thumbnail-size wafer and of sending astronauts to the moon and space probes to Saturn must surely possess the technical knowhow necessary for making a reliable toaster.

According to a law attributed to the savant known only as Murphy, "if anything can go wrong, it will." Corollaries to Murphy's Law suggest themselves as clues to the shoddy goods problem: If anything can break down, it will; if anything can fall apart, it will; if anything can stop running, it will. While Murphy's Law can never be wholly defeated, its effects can usually be postponed. Much of human existence consists of efforts aimed at making sure that things don't go wrong, fall apart, break down, or stop running until a decent interval has elapsed after their manufacture. Forestalling Murphy's Law as applied to products demands intelligence, skill, and commitment. If these human inputs are assisted by special quality-control instruments, machines, and scientific sampling procedures, so much the better. But gadgets and sampling alone will never do the trick since these items are also subject to Murphy's Law. Quality-control instruments need maintenance; gauges go out of order; X rays and laser beams need adjustments. No matter how advanced the technology, quality demands intelligent, motivated human thought and action.

Some reflection about the material culture of prehistoric and preindustrial peoples may help to show what I mean. A single visit to a museum which displays artifacts used by simple preindustrial societies is sufficient to dispel the notion that quality is dependent on technology. Artifacts may be of simple, even primitive design, and yet be built to serve their intended purpose in a reliable manner during a lifetime of use. We acknowledge this when we honor the label "handmade" and pay extra for the jewelry, sweaters, and handbags turned out by the dwindling breeds of modern-day craftspeople.

What is the source of quality that one finds, let us say, in a Pomo Indian basket so tightly woven that it was used to hold boiling water and never leaked a drop, or in an Eskimo skin boat with its matchless combination of lightness, strength, and seaworthiness? Was it merely the fact that these items were handmade? I don't think so. In unskilled or uncaring hands a handmade basket or boat can fall apart as quickly as baskets or boats made by machines. I rather think that the reason we honor the label "handmade" is because it evokes not a technological relationship between producer and product but a social relationship between producer and consumer. Throughout prehistory it was the fact that producers and consumers were either one and the same individuals or close kin that guaranteed the highest degree of reliability and durability in manufactured items. Men made their own spears, bows and arrows, and projectile points; women wove their own baskets and carrying nets, fashioned their own clothing from animal skins, bark, or fiber. Later, as technology advanced and material culture grew more complex, different members of the band or village adopted craft specialties such as pottery-making, basket-weaving, or canoe-building. Although many items were obtained through barter and trade, the connection between producer and consumer still remained intimate, permanent, and caring.

A man is not likely to fashion a spear for himself whose point will fall off in midflight; nor is a woman who weaves her own basket likely to make it out of rotted straw. Similarly, if one is sewing a parka for a husband who is about to go hunting for the family with the temperature at sixty below, all stitches will be perfect. And when the men who make boats are the uncles and fathers of those who sail them, they will be as seaworthy as the state of the art permits.

In contrast, it is very hard for people to care about strangers or about products to be used by strangers. In our era of industrial mass production and mass marketing, quality is a constant problem because the intimate sentimental and personal bonds which once made us responsible to each other and to our products have withered away and been replaced by money relationships. Not only are the producers and consumers strangers but the women and men involved in various stages of production and distribution—management, the worker on the factory floor, the office help, the salespeople—are also strangers to each other. In larger companies there may be hundreds of thousands of people all working on the same product who can never meet face-to-face or learn one another's names. The larger the company and the more complex its division of labor, the greater the sum of uncaring relationships and hence the greater the effect of Murphy's Law. Growth adds layer on layer of executives, foremen, engineers, production workers, and sales specialists to the payroll. Since each new employee contributes a diminished share to the overall production process, alienation from the company and its product are likely to increase along with the neglect or even purposeful sabotage of quality standards.

My basic contention is that after World War II, quality problems reached crisis proportions as a result of the unprecedented increase in the size and complexity of U.S. manufacturing corporations and hence in the quantity of alienated and uncaring workers and managers. This is not to say that only large corporations have quality problems; small companies can also produce shoddy goods but in a free enterprise system they are not likely to remain in business very long. Not only do giant corporations tend to produce alienated workers, managers, and shoddy goods on a giant scale but they tend to stay in business.

Before I present the evidence which links the size and internal organization of U.S. manufacturers to the product-quality problem, let me comment on an objection which is sure to be raised by those familiar with the comparisons now being drawn between Japanese and U.S. products. Many reasons have been offered why Japan was able to overcome America's historic leadership in fields as diverse as automobiles, steel, shipbuilding, pianos, and consumer electronics, but no one has suggested that it was because industry in Japan is less centralized than in the United States. Industrial management is at least as centralized in Japan as in the United States. But the adverse effects of centralization do not necessarily show up at an equal rate or with equal severity in different firms, industries, and countries. In the short run, the formation of giant corporations might even temporarily lead to improvements in product quality. Much depends on the specific historical circumstances characteristic of each country's rise to industrial preeminence. One country's giant corporations can be more or less efficient than another's depending on the kind of competition it faces in the international market, the relative age of its manufacturing facilities, the proportion of its industrial capital devoted to the production of armaments, the proportion of its workforce engaged in services as opposed to manufacturing, and many other variables. I see no reason, therefore, to abandon the theory that America's product-quality problems are the result of the increasing concentration and bureaucratization of American industry merely because the Japanese (or Germans) for the moment possess more efficient giant corporations. The ephemeral nature of the industrial preeminence gained first by Great Britain and then by the United States suggests that industrial success breeds its own downfall. Why should we assume that the Japanese case will be any different? But more on this point later on.

Perhaps, before going further, I should also point out some of the reasons why America's corporations have grown so big. In a free enterprise economy some manufacturers are bound to succeed more than others. Unless the government intervenes, the more successful companies will swallow up the less successful ones. Eventually, if the process were allowed to continue, there might be only one company in each major field, and perhaps ultimately there might even be only one company in the entire country. Congress passed antimonopoly laws early in the century which slowed down the process of concentration and prevented the development of genuine monopolies. But these laws did not prevent the formation of semimonopolies—or what are better known as oligopolies, that is, companies which control not all but a major share of the market for a particular product.

The trend toward oligopoly was already well advanced in the earlier part of this century. But after the end of World War II, the pace of acquisitions and expansions quickened as U.S. companies took advantage of America's new preeminent global status. With most of the other industrial powers crippled by the damage to their factories, American manufacturing companies grew to phenomenal size, developed huge internal bureaucracies, hired hundreds of thousands of workers, earned billions of dollars per year and controlled ever-increasing shares of the national and international markets for an increasingly diverse set of products.

As a result, by 1975 the two hundred largest manufacturing companies had a greater share of all manufacturing, sales, employment, and assets than the largest five hundred had in 1955. Today the fifty largest U.S. manufacturing corporations own 42 percent of all assets used in manufacturing while the top five hundred own 72 percent of these assets. Four or fewer companies dominate 99 percent of the domestic production of cars, 92 percent of flat glass, 90 percent of cereal breakfast foods, 90 percent of turbines and turbine engines, 90 percent of electric lamps, 85 percent of household refrigerators and freezers, 84 percent of cigarettes, 83 percent of television picture tubes, 79 percent of aluminum production and 73 percent of tires and inner tubes.

Moreover, not only have fewer companies come to dominate more of the market for a particular product, but through mergers and acquisitions, an increasing share of all manufacturing is carried out by oligopolistic conglomerates that produce a variety of product lines ranging from tomatoes to oil, from green peas to luggage, and from aluminum to cigarettes. As depicted by *Business Week* magazine in an issue devoted to the "Decline of U.S. Industry," these conglomerates are "multi-product, multi-divisional, multi-locational hydras."

I should mention one other aspect of the post-World War II rise of oligopolies and conglomerates. It is an axiom of the labor movement that industries dominated by a few large corporations are easier to organize than those in which there are hundreds of small companies. As in the auto industry, a strike against one company may be enough to bring the others in line. And so it is no accident that after World War II, national labor unions emerged whose scale and degree of concentration matched those of the principal manufacturing companies. By the mid-1960s therefore, the bulk of America's manufactured items was being produced in giant conglomerate, unionized oligopolies.

In failing to compensate for the loss of the kinds of interests that bound producers and consumers together in preindustrial societies, both labor unions and management contributed to America's post-World War II quality problem. I do not think it is useful or meaningful to say whether one or the other is more to blame for it. In a sense neither is to blame, since both labor and management acted in their own immediate best interest. Did they understand the long-range consequences of what they were doing?

Let me deal with labor's contribution to product-quality

problems first. Because of contracts negotiated during the 1950s and 1960s, management found it increasingly difficult to discipline workers who botched and bungled their tasks or who stayed home from work on the slightest pretext. All contracts involving major manufacturing companies contain provisions that protect workers from being fined or fired without lengthy grievance procedures. Factory workers also have unemployment insurance to fall back on, as a further buffer against managerial pressures. Moreover, today's assembly-line workers are better educated than their predecessors, have higher aspirations, and are more easily bored by the mindless routines that factory work demands. Management complains that if union workers are reprimanded for doing careless or shoddy work, they talk back and take the next day off. Pushed too hard, they may even seek revenge by leaving out a crucial bolt or by dropping a newspaper into the gas tank. New car dealers report a rash of buyers who won't purchase a car unless they know on what day of the week it was made, the theory being that "lemons" are cars that are put together either on Monday or Friday. On Monday, or so the theory goes, the assembly-line workers are hung over from the weekend, many regulars stay home, and their replacements on the line botch the job. Absenteeism is also high on Fridays. Distracted by thoughts of the weekend, even the regulars get sloppy and jam ill-fitting parts together.

Yet the production worker's alienation and antagonism can account for only part of the product-quality problem. Obviously there has to be a separate explanation for product-quality problems that stem from faulty or frivolous design. Responsibility for the gas guzzler's excessive weight, inadequate ventilation, and foldaway wipers, for example, rests with management, not with the ordinary auto worker.

Moreover, despite an increasing volume of complaints during the 1960s, U.S. manufacturers largely ignored the quality issue until foreign firms had penetrated the domestic market. In the case of color television, for example, U.S. manufacturers did not begin to concentrate on improving the reliability and durability of their sets until the Japanese had won a commanding lead—a lead which soon proved fatal to most American firms even though they had been the pioneers of color TV engineering.

According to U.S. quality engineer Joseph Juran, American sets broke down more often because they were designed to operate at higher temperatures than the Japanese sets. Off-the-record information supplied by various company managers indicates that in the mid-1970s American (and other Western) color television sets "were failing in service at a rate five times that prevailing in Japanese sets." Despite recent efforts to narrow this gap, Juran claims that Japanese models are still two to four times more reliable.

I think the best evidence of U.S. management's lack of concern about quality problems is the fact that there are virtually no "life-cycle" data on civilian consumer products. It is from following products through their "life-cycle," from birth to death, under actual conditions of use that manufacturers can learn exactly how often an item breaks down, what kinds of repairs it needs, how much the repairs cost in consumers' time and money, and how long the product can remain in use before the consumer must get rid of it. Because of management's failure to carry out life-cycle product studies, it is no exaggeration to say that not only have consumers been kept in the dark concerning how good a particular product is, but the manufacturers themselves typically are almost as ill-informed as the consumers. To the extent that manufacturers have tried to find out how long their products will last, it is only to make certain that they will not break down during the warranty period. (Telephones and other leased equipment are exceptional in this regard since it is the manufacturer that must bear the cost of replacement.) But even for the warranty period the manufacturers seldom have information on how much the defect will cost the consumer in terms of inconvenience and time and money spent on letters, phone calls, and transportation for traveling back and forth to service centers.

But U.S. manufacturers did more than merely ignore the life-cycle characteristics of their products. They were also simultaneously developing the marketing technique known as "planned obsolescence." As a result, is it not fair to say that shoddiness was not only tolerated but actually welcomed as a means of enhancing short-run profitability? Was it not after World War II that U.S. manufacturers began to bring out annual models of vacuum cleaners, refrigerators, toasters, fans, washers and dryers, blenders, and sewing machines? The list can be extended indefinitely, even to notebooks and paper clips. While these new models sometimes incorporated significant technological advances, such as automatic cycles on washers and dryers, the majority involved cosmetic changes or the attachment of accessory features of dubious value. Vacuum cleaners acquired power-driven wheels; refrigerators were fitted with extra doors, compartments, and trays; toasters got servo-motors that lowered the slice of bread on contact; fans were given thermostats; washers, dryers, and blenders were fitted with rows of dials and control buttons; stoves got timers, clocks, and chromium moldings.

Planned obsolescence exploits the consumer's faith that the newer a product is, the better it will perform. Americans, with their strong emphasis on youth and modernity and their generally optimistic view of the future, were easy targets for this strategy.

Planned obsolescence, of course, is not necessarily the same thing as planned product failure. It is one thing to gull people into believing a new model is "improved" when it is merely new. It is something quite different knowingly to make the new model break down sooner than its predecessors. Not unexpectedly, I found that engineers and designers vigorously deny the existence of planned product failure. Yet one need not invoke a deliberate conspiracy in order to show a connection between planned obsolescence and the epidemic of shoddy American goods.

Who can deny that in the absence of vigorous corrective action, changing models by adding parts will automatically lead to rising rates of product failure? This follows not only from Murphy's Law, but from what engineers regard as the basic principle of quality control, namely that the reliability rate of any device or structure is not the average of, but the product of, the reliability rates of its separate parts. Let me explain. Suppose that a device has two parts, each of which predictably fails on the average in one out of a hundred units per year. Each part then has a reliability rate of .99 per year. But according to the laws of probability the reliability of the device itself will not be .99; rather it will be .99 × .99, which is .98. With ten components rated at .99, the reliability of the product drops to .90 and with one hundred such components it drops to a catastrophic .37. In other words, without a concerted engineering, design, and production effort aimed at compensating for the additions and accessories which were used to create the impression that last year's models had become obsolete, lower product quality becomes a virtual certainty. For example, late model washing machines have 18 to 24 cycles, 10 to 14 pushbuttons, three to five temperature settings and two or three different speeds. "When you add all those up," comments John Petersen, national service manager of Montgomery Ward and Company, "the failure rate has to be higher."

Let us grant that there were probably few instances of top executives actually instructing designers and engineers to make sure that a product would fail by a certain date. More likely management instructed designers and engineers to make sure that a product would *not* fail by a certain date—the date specified in the manufacturer's warranty (or in the case of features that might constitute a safety hazard, the period specified by consumer-product safety laws). So when the product broke down after the guarantee period, technically no one could say that management planned it that way. The verdict then is that if U.S. manufacturers did not actually conspire with their engineers and designers to make things fall apart, their use of planned obsolescence and their neglect of life-cycle quality data achieved the same effect.

As planned obsolescence and neglect steadily lowered product quality, the great reservoir of consumer confidence in products bearing the label "Made in U.S.A." began to run dry. In many product lines, consumers began to see "Made in U.S.A." as a mark of inferior merchandise. By the mid-1970s, proud captains of American industry were down on their knees begging consumers to "Buy American," while pleading with Congress for treasury handouts and tariffs and quotas against foreign imports. What millions of Americans can't understand is why the U.S. managerial elite did nothing about the product-quality problem until they had squandered the immense treasure of confidence which the label "Made in U.S.A." had once enjoyed.

Part of the answer surely lies in the tendency among overgrown, bureaucratic firms for top executives to lose touch with the needs and experiences of their customers. The sheer size of some companies instilled a sense of superhuman invulnerability among the people at the top that weakened their ability to detect and correct mistakes. From former Chevrolet division head John De Lorean's account of his fellow executives at General Motors in the late 1960s, for example, there emerges a picture of executives who were convinced that their empires were eternal. They remind me of the French generals on the Maginot Line or the officers on board the *Titanic*. They thought their corporations were impregnable and unsinkable. Why worry if a few customers complained now and then about being stuck with a "lemon"? De Lorean attributes Detroit's problems to the fact that his fellow chief executive officers were "isolated" from contact with the "real world." He says that they were "unable to accept criticism inside or out," that they were "totalitarian," and that they were deficient in "broad-based understanding and experiences." At a time when customers were crying mightily about poor car quality, service problems, and the unpleasantness often associated with buying a car, "top managers probably haven't purchased a car for themselves or sat in a line outside a dealer's service garage in 20 years." Apparently, G.M.'s top executives were driven about in chauffeured company cars that were serviced daily in special executive garages. These cars were not likely to go dead in the middle of a freeway, leak in a thunderstorm, or rattle as soon as they got off the glass on the showroom floor.

Objectively, what do the relationships between America's top executives and the ordinary consumer remind us of? I cannot help but think of the consumers and high government officials in the Soviet Union. Aren't complaints treated in both countries with that haughty indifference which is the prerogative of commissars? For example, asked to explain why there were no side vent windows in the front doors anymore, a top General Motors executive claimed that "popular opinion" had forced their removal, much like the high-ranking Soviet official who once explained that the price of bread in Moscow had gone up by "popular demand."

There is another aspect of America's corporate empires to be considered. Post-World War II managerial attitudes toward quality must have been heavily influenced by the rise of conglomerates as the dominant form of U.S. business enterprise. The reason is that many conglomerates are not only or even primarily in the business of producing goods; they are in the business of buying and selling companies. The point is that knowhow needed to buy and sell companies is different from the knowhow needed to produce a line of high-quality products. "All too often," comments *Business Week,* today's executives "see themselves as managers of a portfolio of companies much like a portfolio of stocks. They become more concerned with buying and selling companies than with selling improved products to consumers." A study by a West Coast consulting firm concludes that most U.S. executives "have never participated in the line management process" and warns that we will "have to see a shift in the background of top executives to technical and operating skills because [now their] attention never goes beyond financial reports." But the opposite trend is still in the ascendancy. "Large corporations

32

have been virtually overrun by a proliferation of profit-zealous MBAs [holders of Masters of Business Administration degrees from business schools] who are trained to tighten every operation to get 'good quarterly numbers,' " and who have little interest in the effects of their activities several years hence. By then they hope to have been hired by another conglomerate.

Insiders agree that there is something very different in the way today's executives relate to their corporations which sets them off from an earlier generation of business leaders. De Lorean, for example, characterized them as "short-term professional managers" who stay with a company for less than ten years and who are dominated by the need to produce immediate profits during their short term in office. In keeping with their frequent movement from one corporation to another, their wealth no longer consists primarily of stock in the company they work for, and so they don't have to worry about what will happen if, let us say, their firm's reputation for quality collapses shortly after they leave it. Richard Barnet and Ronald Müller foresaw in their book *Global Reach* that the new breed of "money managers and marketing specialists" would have "little direct interest or pride in their products" and would be unlikely to display a "passion for quality or craftsmanship."

Conglomerates spent more than forty billion dollars on acquisitions in 1979. What did this do for the quality of goods made in U.S.A.? James B. Farley, chairman of the business consulting firm of Booz, Allen and Hamilton, estimates that as often as not acquisitions do nothing that benefits anyone as far as production is concerned. And one can only guess at the damage acquisitions do to product quality by arbitrarily shifting personnel and by making executives anxious about job security. When a big company swallows a little one, the big executives invariably swear to the little executives that no one will be fired. But it is hard to sit at one's desk knowing there is an alligator in the corridor.

33

Doesn't all this buying and selling of companies go a long way toward explaining why many manufacturers have been willing to compromise their firm's reputation for quality at the risk of ruining its good name? After all, there is an excellent chance that within five years the company will not have the same name anymore or that it will be marketing a line of products bearing some other company's "good name." In fact many manufacturing conglomerates have names which few Americans have ever heard of. For example, Easy-Off Oven Cleaner, Brach's Milk Chocolate, Black Flag Ant Killer, Woolite, Anacin, and Chef Boy-Ar-Dee are well known TV brand names and companies. But I wonder how many people who buy these brands have heard of the American Home Products Corporation of 685 Third Avenue, New York City, which is the name of the conglomerate that manufactures all of these items?

People in the know say that the regurgitation and reswallowing of companies by conglomerates also offers creative finance-oriented chief executives many possibilities for improving the parent firm's economic position. Acquired firms with good profit records help conglomerates with poor profit records look good on the annual statement. "The result, at least until the investors catch on, is a rise in the value of the parent company's stock greater than would be justified by the profits of the company alone." Conversely, acquisitions of firms showing losses may be intended primarily as an income tax strategy. Having served their purpose, one out of six U.S. firms acquired by conglomerates goes out of business. Through various ingenious feats of accountancy, the parent company often finds it advantageous to run acquisitions into the ground, deliberately lowering the quality of a famous brand and ruining its national reputation in return for windfall profits. Stanley E. Cohen of *Advertising Age* warned in 1971 that "So many brands have been debauched as they pass from one conglomerate to another that the number of consumers who trust them is shrinking. Brands are born and killed with such facility these days that consumers are constantly reminded that sellers themselves put little value in them."

And let us not forget that America's manufacturing giants command huge advertising budgets. This is another reason why it was so easy for management to tolerate or even encourage the decline in the quality of U.S. products. Rather than trying to do something about alienated labor, planned obsolescence, and the absence of product life-cycle data, manufacturers seem to have found that it was easier or cheaper to launch commercial propaganda campaigns aimed at convincing the consumer that U.S. products were getting better every year. In formulating their advertising strategies, manufacturers assiduously followed H. L. Mencken's advice that "no one ever lost money by underestimating the intelligence of the average American." I think events have proved that this advice is well taken only in the short run; thereafter one would do better heeding Lincoln's admonition that "you can't fool all of the people all of the time."

Finally, and perhaps overriding all of the other reasons why U.S. management tolerated or even encouraged the production of shoddy goods, there remains the matter of oligopoly controls over the market. Manufacturers tend to lose their sense of alarm over the long-range effects of their policies if consumers can purchase an item needed to maintain their accustomed way of life from among only three or four companies (all of which are simultaneously yielding to the temptation to debauch the quality of their latest models). Once an oligopoly situation has developed, management is at liberty to disregard consumer complaints. The handful of companies that dominate a particular market face similar problems and tend to solve them by taking similar measures. Just as such companies tend to raise their prices at the same time (as will be seen later on), so too they tend to lower quality at the same time. Where oligopoly reigns therefore, managers have both the incentive and the means to compensate for the apathy and hostility of their employees, and for their own bureaucratic boondoggling, by letting quality deteriorate under the cloak of model changeovers and hundred-million-dollar ad campaigns.

As I mentioned earlier, there is a confusing aspect of the uproar over U.S. product-quality problems that I don't want to overlook. The Japanese have had the greatest success in penetrating the U.S. market by exporting reliable and durable cars, TV sets, tape recorders, radios, cameras, and record players. Yet aren't Japan's manufacturing firms at least as highly oligopolized and conglomerated as America's "multi-product, multi-divisional, multi-locational hydras"? I admit that the success of "Japan Inc." in the product-quality field suggests that there is room for management and labor to improve America's quality ratings despite the built-in constraints and temptations of oligopolized and bureaucratic corporate structures. We know that the Japanese government and managerial elite have fashioned a workplace environment and a social support system that favor the development of feelings of loyalty instead of alienation. In the largest firms, workers enjoy lifetime job security, pensions at fifty-five, and comprehensive company-subsidized medical and social services. And on the factory floor, Japanese workers are organized into small production teams whose members have collective responsibility for product quality and are rewarded with semiannual bonuses based on the team's performance.

Apparently, some aspects of the Japanese system can be transferred to Western cultures. For example, under American management, the Motorola Company was producing television sets with an average of 150 to 180 defects for each one hundred sets packed and ready for shipment. Three years later under Japanese management and the new name Quasar, with the same group of American workers still on the assembly line, the "fall-off" rate was down to three or four per hundred sets, or about one-fortieth of its previous level. All this may be true, but the specific history of Japan's rise to quality eminence must be kept in mind before anyone denies that there is a causal relationship between the size and degree of concentration of U.S. manufacturers and the epidemic of U.S. product-quality problems. After World War II, as a vanquished power with a long-standing reputation for exporting junk, Japan embarked upon a comprehensive plan to develop a new image. Exports had to pass rigorous government inspection before they could be shipped. As the underdog, Japan consciously instituted a national crusade to become number one in product quality. No major managerial decisions could be made which did not give top priority to improving national product quality standards. Moreover, Japan's managerial elite could scarcely engage in the buying and selling of companies and the debauchery of brand names as a means of making quick profits. In order to make money from selling one's reputation, one must have a reputation to sell. As far as quality was concerned, the Japanese had no place to go but up.

Their postwar recovery rested on their ability to export manufactured goods. Hence they had to overcome their reputation for shoddy goods if they were to penetrate foreign markets. It remains to be seen how long they will be able to resist the temptations to reap short-term rewards now that they have achieved their primary objective. It also remains to be seen how long they will be able to maintain their vaunted company paternalism and manager-worker solidarity now that they have vanquished their international competitors and as the sense of national purpose becomes diluted by the inevitable frictions of class and rank. For example, a fateful bridge that Japan has yet to cross is the integration of female workers into its mainstream labor force. Japanese women earn at a rate that is less than half what men earn and many of the lowest and most menial functions in Japan are fulfilled by older married women. To a considerable extent the price advantage of Japanese products rests ultimately on the virtually unchecked exploitation of cheap female labor. It remains to be seen how long this submerged half of Japanese society will accept its traditional submissive status and its meager share of Japan Inc.'s success.

In rushing to Japan to discover how the Japanese got the better of them in the international market, American managers seem to be forgetting that there is a domestic as well as an international standard against which product quality can be measured. The main problem as the American consumer sees it is not that Japan has risen to industrial preeminence but that the quality of American-made goods seems to have deteriorated. In concentrating on finding out why the Japanese have beaten them, American managers may be running away from the more important question of why they let U.S. product quality decline.

It is futile to speculate about how much of the U.S. product-quality decline could have been avoided had U.S. oligopolies instituted Japanese-style managerial practices and product-quality incentives and controls in the 1960s. The fact is that they did not. Let us turn instead to the connections between the onset of the product-quality problem and the other startling changes in the American way of life. We need to pay special attention to the relationship between a general decline in the quality of goods and the rise in the cost of living. Is it not a form of inflation if consumers find that more and more of the things they have just bought break down, fall apart, and need to be repaired? It seems to me that a country that lets Murphy's Law take over a bigger share of the economy each year has an inflation going even if prices remain level. But I think that I will be able to explain this point more clearly after we take a look at the causes of the second kind of quality problem that is rampant in America today.

3

Why
the Help
Won't Help
You

The malady is not confined to any class, sex, race, or religion. It affects everyone and seems to be spreading everywhere. It could happen while you're on a commuter train in Westchester. The air conditioning isn't working and the heat is intolerable. The conductor moves leisurely through the car, collecting tickets.

"Nope, I guess it's not working," he says with a shrug when the passengers complain. But he continues to collect tickets. Ten minutes elapse while the passengers squirm and wipe their brows. At last, the conductor walks casually over to a panel on the wall, flicks a switch, and the blower begins to pump fresh chilled air.

You drive into a "full-service" filling station in Virginia and ask the attendant to check under the hood.

"Who, me?" he asks.

"Yes, you."

So he checks the oil, wipes the dipstick on his uniform, and says: "You're down a quart."

"Okay, give me some."

"We don't have any."

You can get a dose in the supermarket. The young man stacking boxes of cereals doesn't know which aisle the apple-sauce is on: "Ask the manager."

"Where's the manager?"

"He's not here today."

Government is a high-risk area. A seventy-two-year-old man applies for a new Social Security benefit. The clerk says that it will take two years before he gets the first check. When the senior citizen remarks that he might not live that long, the clerk replies: "Don't worry, it will be paid to your estate."

Department stores are another high-risk area. The sales help no longer find the customers. The customers must find the sales help. An experienced shopper learns to look for telltale signs: Sometimes it's a man lurking in a far corner; or it may be a woman without a handbag walking slowly by; or perhaps it's a figure permanently stooped behind a distant counter. Finding three or four people chatting and laughing in the middle of the room won't solve the problem.

"Can anyone help me, please?"

"Sorry, we don't work in this section."

Woe to the customer who presumes a small fund of extra knowledge about the items or services that the employee is handling.

"Can you tell me if this paint is washable?"

"It says on the label."

"Where does it say that?"

"I don't know, mister. I only work here."

Forms of unhelpfulness range from subtle evasion to open hostility. A young woman is standing near the register, arms folded, leaning against a partition. When the customer asks her for help, she replies frankly: "I was supposed to have my coffee break fifteen minutes ago. I'm not going to wait on anybody until after my break."

Understandably, abuses of clients and customers that violate civil or criminal statutes get the greatest attention from consumer advocates. Each year negligence, malpractice, and breach-of-contract cases involving service personnel clog the courts. There's reckless driving by bus drivers, malpractice by doctors, food poisoning by caterers, kickbacks by officials, even assaults by irate filling station attendants. But most instances of client or customer abuse do not result in actionable injuries, and consumer advocates have tended to overlook them as mere inconveniences. The ability of these mere inconveniences to destroy the victim's well-being should not be underestimated. As will be seen in a moment from the files in a consumer complaint agency, there is an immense squandering of time and energy, and great rage and frustration engendered by the misinformation and disservices that are rampant in America today.

The problems created by the epidemic of misinformation and disservices probably should be regarded as a greater menace to the American dream than the epidemic of shoddy goods. My reason for saying this is that service-and-information production has in many ways become a more important focus of the U.S. economy than goods production. Since 1947 service-and-information jobs have been expanding almost ten times faster than manufacturing jobs. Today, people-processing and information-processing jobs outnumber goods-producing jobs by at least two to one.

We began our inquiry into the causes of product-quality problems by asking how higher standards were achieved in former times. The same procedure seems appropriate in the matter of the quality of information and services and in fact, historically, the conditions responsible for quality in one are very similar to those responsible for quality in the other. While skill and technology count, the decisive factor in both instances is the nature of the social bonds between producer and consumer. What most assured quality services in the past was that server and served knew each other and were personally interested in each other's welfare. Services rendered by members of small preindustrial societies or by members of the same family met this specification in quintessential form. Within their spheres of competence one cannot be better served than by lifelong neighbors and close kin. As in the case of goods production, the further one gets from the small-scale intimacy of the family, village, or neighborhood, the more likely one is to encounter services that are inappropriate or inadequate because of the absence of personalized and motivated relationships.

Virtually all of the new jobs added to the American economy during the transition from goods production to service-and-information production are of the sort that are deficient in personalized and motivated relationships. The businesses and government agencies responsible for hiring most of the new service-and-information personnel have mainly been large-scale bureaucratic organizations in which workers serve customers and clients who are complete strangers and who see each other only once in a lifetime. In addition, since service-and-information workers fall within the lowest-paid segment of the labor force, for reasons to be clarified later on, their training has been kept to a minimum and many remain only marginally competent to carry out their duties.

With increasing frequency, disinterest and incompetence combined to create misinformation and disservices whose impact can be described only as catastrophic. No one knows how many of these catastrophes are inflicted on consumers each year, but they have become a familiar feature of contemporary American life. (I do not mean to imply that America is the only country that produces catastrophic disservices and catastrophic misinformation. There is reason to believe that they occur in every bureaucratized and oligopolized economy.) Let me give an example that is on file in the Consumer Affairs Division of the Law and Public Safety Department of the State of New Jersey: Mrs. Brown (which is not her real name) ordered four denim-blue matching sectional pieces of furniture—two sofas and two loveseats—from a suburban branch of one of the largest department stores in the country. Three months after the purchase date a deliveryman appeared with one sofa instead of two. While he had brought the correct number of loveseats, one had a hole in it and Mrs. Brown had to send it back. Three months later—six months from purchase—another deliveryman brought a midnight-blue sofa and a sky-blue loveseat with midnight-blue cushions which not only didn't match each other but didn't match the denim-blue sofa and loveseat already in the living room. Mrs. Brown sent both pieces back, contacted an employee, and was told that the store would send four new sections so that there would be no further mismatches. After a month, Mrs. Brown received a postcard advising her to be prepared to accept delivery of three (not four) pieces of furniture—two sofas and a loveseat. Phoning again, she reached another employee who advised her to accept the three pieces and then call the store to complain afterward. When the three pieces arrived (a week later than the delivery date), the two sofas turned out to be different colors again and the loveseat again had a hole in it. Mrs. Brown had in the meantime gone ahead and purchased new drapes and carpeting to match the denim-blue furniture, so she called the store yet another time and yet another employee again promised four new matching pieces. Another deliveryman brought not four but one piece and that one piece also had a hole in it. Finally she spoke to a Ms. Jay (not her real name) who committed the store—for the third time—to order four new pieces from the manufacturer. Wrote Mrs. Brown:

That was six months ago. Now Ms. Jay contacted me and said there's been a mistake. Instead of special-ordering four pieces she said that they had special-ordered three and would I accept that? I explained the whole problem to her and would you believe, she said she'd re-order four pieces for a July 1979 delivery date [two years after the original purchase!].

But when Ms. Jay tried to place the order, the manufacturer announced that the fabric had been discontinued. While all of this was going on, the store kept billing Mrs. Brown for the completed purchase and "twice closed my account and turned it over to a collection agency, despite my letter of explanation."

The disservice to Mrs. Brown reached catastrophic proportions because each additional employee whom she contacted neither knew her personally nor had the slightest idea about what had already transpired. At each encounter Mrs. Brown had to start her story from the beginning and with each retelling it grew longer and longer as if she had gotten caught in an "Old MacDonald Had a Farm" roundelay. Bureaucratic effects permeate the saga. Each order started out sound and whole and then as it got passed along from office to office it was garbled somewhere down the line, no one knew where. And as we saw, one employee actually felt so dominated by bureaucratic routines that she could only advise Mrs. Brown not to interrupt a delivery they both knew would be unsatisfactory, but to let it happen, and then complain through regular channels.

The characteristics of the service-and-information-producing jobs added to the economy since 1945 have had a great deal to do with the increasing importance of disservices in American life. Since service-and-information workers are white-collar employees we tend to think of them as being among the better-paid members of the workforce. The facts are otherwise. Well over half—56 percent—of service-and-information producing jobs fall within the low-level earnings segment of the labor market. Twenty-seven percent fall within the medium level while only 17 percent are in the upper level. This is in sharp contrast to the earning-segment distribution of goods-producing jobs. Only a third of goods-producing jobs are low-level, 40 percent are medium level, and 26 percent are upper level. "Clearly, the most striking finding regarding employment in the services is that workers are engaged to a disproportionate extent in low-income activities" writes economist and service expert Thomas Stanback.

Service-and-information workers, in keeping with their low wages, also tend to be younger, to work only part time and to change jobs frequently. For reasons to be discussed in another chapter, women now hold half of all service-and-information jobs. Unfortunately three-quarters of their jobs are low-income jobs.

In the retail trades for example, where earnings are only half of the national median, there has recently been a rise in the percent of female sales help (from 45 to 56 percent), a rise in the proportion of workers less than twenty-five years old (from 27 percent to 40 percent), and a rise in the proportion of part-time workers (from 29 percent to 35 percent). Half of the women now employed in retail trades have held the same jobs for less than eighteen months.

Many part-time and temporary service-and-information workers do not get any training at all. For example, Louise Kapp Howe, the author of *Pink Collar Workers* (1977), once took a job as a temporary salesperson selling women's coats in Gimbels. To teach her the location of the various styles and sizes of coats, the department's manager made one right turn around the room vaguely pointing toward distant racks. Thereupon Howe was unleashed upon a customer who was looking for a "black cashmere coat, size eighteen."

Facing a room filled with rack after rack of garments, style and size unknown, Howe led the customer to a section that had fur-trimmed coats.

"Not fur-trimmed. Cashmere. Plain black cashmere," said the disbelieving customer. Howe and the customer continued to wander from rack to rack until another employee intervened and assured them both that the store did not carry cashmere coats.

Later Howe interviewed a more experienced employee. "How do you like selling?" she asked. The employee, who had a foreign accent, replied: "What you mean selling? This is not selling." She explained the difference:

> Selling is when it matters how you and your customers get to know each other, how you help her find what's best, how you understand what she needs. Here you no sell. Lady comes in, asks for something, you go find it, she buys or she no buys, that's it, you never see her no more. That's not selling. That's showing.

I find it rather ironic that the transformation of the United States economy from goods-production to service-and-information-production has been widely hailed as the end of industrial society and the coming of the "post-industrial" age. Supposedly post-industrial society is emerging out of industrial society just as industrial society once emerged out of agricultural society. During the nineteenth and early twentieth centuries, farm jobs dwindled while factory jobs rose; today service jobs rise while factory jobs dwindle. "What is clear," writes sociologist Daniel Bell, "is that if an industrial society is defined as a goods-producing society—if manufacture is central in shaping the character of its labor force—then the United States is no longer an industrial society." But I think Bell and the other post-industrial enthusiasts have been misled by the notion that white-collar work is different from blue-collar work—that people-processing and information-processing are more prestigious, brainier, better paid, and less arduous activities than tightening bolts on an assembly line. This idea bears little relationship to the actual nature of service jobs and to their effect on the character of the labor force, now or in the foreseeable future.

The actual jobs performed by today's service-and-information personnel closely resemble the jobs in Adam Smith's famous description of an eighteenth-century pin factory. According to Smith, the essence of the industrial division of labor is that "distinct hands" perform distinct operations: "One man draws out the wire, another straightens it, a third

46

cuts it, a fourth points it, a fifth grinds it at the top for receiving the head," and so forth, down to the man who inserts the pins into their paper wrapping. When services are produced by "distinct hands" carrying out separate operations, we have industrialized services, not post-industrial society. In any large modern business office, for example, separate clerks open the mail, others date and route the orders, others clear credit, others check the items to see if they are in inventory, still others type the invoice, add prices to it, subtract the discount, calculate shipping fees, and dispatch the item to the customer. Moreover, as Harry Braverman emphasizes in his book, *Labor and Monopoly Capital,* this detailed division of tasks leads to the separation of mental from physical operations and of management from labor just as it does in the factory.

> Just as in manufacturing processes . . . the work of the office is analyzed and parcelled out among a great many detail workers, who now lose all comprehension of the process as a whole and the policies which underlie it. The special privilege of the clerk of old, that of being witness to the operation of the enterprise as a whole . . . disappears. Each of the activities requiring interpretation of policy or contact beyond the department or section becomes the province of a higher functionary.

One of the advancing frontiers of the de-skilling of service-and-information workers lies in the restaurant business. As the fast-food chains take over, they do away with the need for qualified cooks and chefs, personalized menus, knowledgeable waiters, waitresses, and stewards. Enter "equipment and products designed to be operated (or sold) by minimally trained, unskilled persons, of whom high turnover rates are expected," namely part-timers whose jobs consist of sorting out boxed uniform portions of food prepared and frozen off-premises and of serving them without frills (clean your own table).

Simple, dull, routinized, repetitive tasks carried out in offices, schools, or hospitals have the same effect on the psychology of the worker as simple, dull, routinized, repetitive tasks carried out in factories. In both instances the workers become bored, disinterested, and alienated from the product whether it be a manufactured good or a service. True, when Karl Marx first set forth the symptomology of alienation in 1844 he had factory workers in mind, but that was simply because there were as yet few large-scale routinized information-processing and people-processing jobs in the private economy, and government service work (except for the army) was still very rudimentary.

Industrialized white- and pink-collar workers can become just as alienated as factory workers. In fact one could argue that the earliest cases of alienated labor probably occurred not among Adam Smith's workers in a pin factory but among the low-level scribes and functionaries in the government bureaucracies that were characteristic of the ancient civilizations of China and of the Middle East. Government bureaus and offices in which distinct hands performed distinct operations existed long before the invention of the steam engine or the assembly line.

This point tends to be overlooked by the soothsayers of post-capitalist society as much as by the soothsayers of post-industrial society. For example, Harry Braverman claims that the detailed division of labor and the antagonism between management and labor are intrinsic features of capitalist but not of socialist societies. The spread of alienation to office work and other non–goods-producing jobs results in his view from the tendency of capitalist firms to subordinate the organization of work and the worker's well-being to the quest for profits. As capitalism matures, it spreads the same kind of labor organization to every nook and cranny of the economy, eventually embracing everything from dating services to fast-food restaurants. In contrast, under socialism, claims Braverman, it is possible to enjoy the benefits of industrial mass production and at the same time to reorganize the work process to eliminate the invidious separation between management and workers as well as the drudgery of the detailed division of labor. Yet even Braverman admits that no modern nation has as yet moved in that direction, least of all the members of the Soviet bloc where the organization of labor still "differs little from the organization of labor in capitalist countries." Since the evidence of the moment clearly shows that the detailed division of labor under a managerial elite is at least as well-developed in industrial socialist societies as in industrial capitalist societies, there would seem to be no justification for supposing that the spread of these features to office work and other services is to be explained only in terms of the specific processes of the monopoly phase of capitalism. We would do well to bear in mind the fact that the most gigantic application of the pin factory model to office work in the U.S.A. is embodied in the federal bureaucracy whose bottom line has seldom been known to be constrained by the need to show a profit (with consequences to be discussed in the next chapter).

An earlier generation of social theorists was fond of predicting that the division of labor in industrial society would lead to a higher form of social bonding. Against Marx who foretold that the division of labor would result in a class war between workers and capitalists, turn-of-the-century sociologist Émile Durkheim and his followers argued that industrialization would lead to the "organic" unity of social life. Instead of society splitting apart as a result of the antagonistic interest of its different classes and occupational groups, it would be held together more firmly than ever—since everyone was becoming dependent upon everyone else—like the body's eyes, hands, heart, and so forth.

So far, Durkheim has turned out to be right about industrial society not splitting apart along class lines, but his idea that the industrial division of labor would result in a more solidaristic form of social life bears as little resemblance to the actual course of events as Marx's vision of class war followed by a classless utopia. It seems to me that both Marx and Durk-heim failed to see that the potential for people to harm each other would increase as a result of the spread of the detailed division of labor to the service-and-information jobs. Actually, alienation can have far more serious consequences when it afflicts certain kinds of service-and-information workers than when it occurs among factory hands. Alienated service-and-information workers can scar, deform, and kill both psycho-logically and physically. Alienated doctors, nurses, and hos-pital workers, for example, raise the incidence of physically damaging malpractice. They send mothers home with the wrong babies, let emergency room patients bleed to death while waiting to have their insurance verified, operate on the wrong patients, and take out the wrong organs—all widely publicized recent incidents. They also make millions of more fortunate people feel small and helpless by treating them like so many sticks of wood or bolts of cloth.

The Congressional Committee on Consumer Affairs esti-mates that motorists throw away ten billion dollars a year on faulty auto repairs. How many more billions of dollars are thrown away on faulty teachers who either don't care or don't know how to make their lessons work? Who can put a price on the psychological and social damage wrought by cata-strophic disservices of our bureaucratized and impersonalized schools and colleges?

Early in the postwar period, service-and-information worker alienation was partially forestalled by the prestige at-tached to working in an office or a store. But as service-and-information jobs became more routinized and more and more women were hired, the snob appeal of service-and-information sector employment began to wear off. Service-and-informa-tion workers started to think of unions and unions started to think of service workers, and this brought new and urgent incentives for the further industrialization of service-and-in-formation jobs and a sharp rise in the incidence of catastrophic misinformation and disservices.

The managers of service-and-information production responded to unionization and rising labor costs exactly as in manufacturing. Having pushed the detailed division of labor to the point where workers were performing highly routinized and machinelike functions, they took the next step of substituting machines for human beings. This sequence has gone furthest in the information-processing fields with the introduction of video display terminals, automated editing and copying typewriters, optical scanners for filing, facsimile transmissions, electronic mail, and automated billing and accounting machines incorporating advanced microchip computer technology.

Before Citibank automated its facilities it took three days, thirty processing steps, and fourteen people working with six files to prepare a letter of credit. After automation one individual seated at a complete "cockpit-like" data-processing work station was able to complete the job the same day the request was received.

Automation enthusiasts contend that the electronic office "will ease the drudgery usually found in America's paper factories . . . by creating more stimulating careers for office workers." According to management, "The individual who used to be a clerk with a green eyeshade is now, at Citibank, a first rate professional whose job equates to the institution's mission." Some office workers will undoubtedly find themselves upgraded by the new technology. A former "green eyeshade" clerk at Citibank, for example, had nothing but praise for the new system:

> Maybe automation puts some people out of work, but it only puts them out of boring work. It's given me a better job, more responsible.

But for the majority of secretarial and clerical workers, climbing into cockpits and getting hooked up to a computer has not been very upgrading. On the contrary, the evidence clearly indicates that white-collar automation has already led to an increase in the detailed division of labor, to the elimination of most of the interesting and versatile secretarial positions, and to a further downgrading of skills and wages. A 1977 study of five large firms by sociologists Evelyn Glenn and Roslyn Feldberg concluded that automated clerical jobs were more mechanical and narrow, and that "the main avenues for clerical workers were either horizontal or downward." Karen Nussbaum of the National Association of Office Workers writes that

> Office automation as it is being introduced today requires that a great many people tediously enter the data, push the right buttons, fill out forms "for the computer" with perfect accuracy, and feed the forms to the computer. Each worker must discipline herself [sic] to the system imposed by the machine. Most often, clericals work with computer terminals which have been strictly programmed to perform only one task.

Seated in a modular cockpit, hooked up to the computer, eyes glued to the video display terminal, the automated office worker is even more likely to become bored, apathetic, alienated, than the pre-automated office worker. The machines themselves supervise and discipline their operators, virtually eliminating contact and conversation with other workers except those who perform similar functions nearby. Reports one video-display-terminal typist:

> There are panels six feet high around all the operators. We're divided into workgroups of 4 to 6 with a supervisor for each workgroup. In many cases we don't see another person all day except for a ten-minute coffee break and lunch time. All we see is the walls around us and sometimes the supervisor. The isolation is terrible.

One German study found that video-display-terminal typists experienced twice as much fatigue, alienation, monotony, and lack of challenge in their jobs as traditional clerical workers. Several other studies link the use of video display terminals to eyestrain, migraine headaches, lower- and upper-back strain, and stress.

Despite a lot of cultlike futurist notions about "third wave electronic cottages" in which after breakfast white-collar employees contentedly slip into their basement cockpit module, turn on the video display terminal, and get to work without ever leaving home, the computer shows no sign of reducing the alienation of industrialized service-and-information workers in the foreseeable future.

Automation will probably soon begin to slow the rate of growth of the service-and-information-producing labor force (a point to which I shall return in the final chapter). But expect no decrease in the *percentage* of arrogant room clerks and snarling theater ticket–sellers, information operators with foreign accents who can't spell, hostesses who keep you waiting for a table while they chat, unreliable and unrepentant postmen and repairmen, evasive low-level administrators, and don't-ask-me-mister-I-only-work-here sales help.

From typists to telephone operators, from stock clerks to mail sorters, automation means progressively less to know and less to think. By using optical scanning machines, file clerks can dispense with knowing the sequence of the alphabet. Supermarket cashiers no longer have to know how to add or subtract. Airline reservationists no longer need know anything about timetables. From lofty functionary upon whose honesty, skill, and acumen the survival of the bank depended, tellers have already become lowly appendages of the bank's central computer, "mere checkout clerks at a money supermarket."

So rampant is this computer-assisted drive to give Adam Smith's pinhead maker a white collar that even futurist Alvin Toffler can fit it into his notions of things to come only by consoling us with the thought that illiterates will feel more at home in the future than they do today. Since paychecks will no longer be linked to the ability to read,

Airline reservation clerks, stock-room personnel, machine operators, and repairmen may be able to function quite adequately on the job by listening rather than reading, as a voice from the machine tells them, step by step, what to do next or how to replace a broken part.

As long as automation does not enhance service-and-information workers' motivation to be helpful, lowers their competence rather than raises it, and locks them into a set of rigid bureaucratic procedures which eliminate the possibility of adapting to novel or atypical situations, the quality of services and information will continue to decline. Somewhere, at input or output or in between, service-and-information-producing machines, like goods-producing machines, need people to run them and maintain them. And so, with each fresh advance in automation, heralded always as the beginning of a new era of easy living, the scope and intensity of disservice and misinformation has increased. Instead of raising the quality of services and information, automation has only succeeded in creating new lopsided links of dependency between unsuspecting customers and clients, and alienated workers, with powerful potentials for causing distress, inconvenience, and frustration.

The computerization of consumer credit accounts, for example, left millions of unsuspecting people vulnerable to bored data processors who could turn one's life upside down with a mere punch of a button. On request, and without the consumers' knowledge, nationwide consumer credit rating companies furnish banks and department stores with the credit history of people applying for loans, mortgages, and credit cards. These companies obtain their information from previous credit grantors and from court records of salary garnisheeings, judgments, and bankruptcies.

Erroneous reports arise in many ways. The clerk making the request for information from the store or credit card company may make an error in the consumer's Social Security number. The credit company's computer may then spew out the record of someone who has a similar name and similar number. Or the credit company personnel themselves may make incorrect entries. By the time the consumer finds out that a mistake has been made, considerable damage has been done and much effort will be needed to get someone to expunge the data from the computer's memory:

> Since 1973 they have carried false information in my files, sending it out to companies on request, and I never knew about it. They promised swift action. I called them to see what a month and a half of their swift action had produced and a secretary told me, after putting me on hold for fifteen minutes, that my file was being reprogrammed by their computer people and that I would hear from them in the future. God only knows what they are programming about me now.

The same company did this to Mr. D.M.: Shortly after he purchased a used car with a bank loan for $2,200, the car was destroyed in an accident. His insurance company estimated the loss at $800 and paid that sum directly to the bank. D.M. dutifully continued to pay off the installments on the remainder of the loan to the bank. However, the bank suddenly went bankrupt. The Federal Deposit Insurance Corporation took it over, demanded immediate payment in full from D.M., sued him when he was unable to come up with the money, and successfully garnisheed his salary. The fact that his salary was garnisheed immediately went into his file at the credit company although the circumstances responsible for it did not. Now he cannot get credit anywhere. I am afraid that Toffler's "third wave" is already here for people like D.M.: "They say this will be on my file for seven years. I cannot take that. Please help."

During the 1960s and 1970s computerized account and record keeping in the hands of apathetic, incompetent, and bureaucratized personnel lowered costs for many government agencies and companies, but raised costs for countless consumers who were billed for things they sent back, never bought, or never received. Department stores are a particularly hellish battleground in the lopsided war between clerks armed with computers that can spew out a thousand threatening letters a minute and defenseless customers and clients who don't even own a typewriter.

"Please help!" begins a typical letter about computer-mediated abuses in a consumer agency's files. "I am being threatened to pay $128 on my account or I will be placed on a national delinquent debtor list." The writer claims she owes nothing. She has called the store repeatedly and made numerous in-person visits trying to find out about the charge but she still does not know what it was for. The pattern recurs in case after case:

> They want me to pay finance charges but I didn't receive any bills. The person I spoke to was very rude. She hung up on me.

> I've written your Philadelphia office twice, and Newark office once and I spoke to one of your people by phone. I received nothing but escalating bills. Then I got a yellow slip saying the account was closed. I don't need this frustration. . . .

> As of this date I have not received a reply to my correspondence. I again state that I have no record of a purchase for the amount in question. I have requested that you either correct my account or send me proof of purchase. This has been to no avail. . . .

> Every effort I have made to straighten the mess out, either by phone or in writing, has been unsuccessful. Your personnel are unresponsive. . . .

How often do computer billing disservices actually occur? In a study carried out by T. D. Sterling of the Department of Computing Science at Simon Fraser University, 40 percent of the respondents in a sample of middle-class consumers detected errors or had complaints about the way their computerized accounts had been handled in the previous twelve months. The most common form of complaint concerned billing errors in which customers or clients detected charges for a nonexistent purchase or found that they had not been properly credited for payments made on account. The most frequent offenders were department stores, credit card companies, utility companies, and mail-order businesses in that order. Most of the people in Sterling's sample succeeded in getting their grievances taken care of by spending an average of two-and-a-half hours working at it and by waiting an average of eight weeks for results. But an unlucky 20 percent had to spend over twenty hours and had to wait more than twenty weeks. In trying to straighten things out, many respondents reported that they had been treated as "troublemakers" and threatened with a loss of their credit rating. In 10 percent of the cases it took extra effort to remove incorrect interest charged on top of incorrect billing charges. Customers or clients who finally succeeded in proving that they had been innocent victims universally complained of being met by an "icy silence." Sterling ends his report with some chilling remarks about the current push toward the creation of paperless electronic data systems:

> From the frequency with which individuals encounter errors and from observing the difficulty with which these errors are corrected, the question naturally comes to mind what will happen when the visible audit trail, such as checks, bills, and receipts, is replaced by electronic signals?

As sociologist Benjamin D. Singer has remarked, the next generation may never know what it was once like to call or write a government agency or a business firm and feel certain that a responsible answer would be forthcoming. As service-and-information production becomes more industrialized, concentrated, bureaucratized, and automated, more and more service-and-information-producing organizations begin to operate behind what might be called one-way communication mirrors. They know who you are; they ship to you; they bill you; they call you; they threaten you. But you don't know who they are. "Case after case," writes Singer, "reveals the same kind of experience. Individuals call, write, appear in person, and are cut off, cannot make contact, are ignored or cannot make their way through labyrinthine channels."

Counting unheeded telephone calls, letters, and postcards, an organization like New York's Consolidated Edison electric company has been known to bounce off or "lose" over a million communications from its customers per year. Many organizations deliberately play hide-and-seek with customers and clients: Supermarkets use unlisted phone numbers; a giant delivery firm leaves notices of intended deliveries but no number to call if the date is inconvenient; warranties have impressive green scrollwork around the edges but not the manufacturer's phone number or address. Some organizations deliberately install "delay circuits"—the dialer hears the phone ringing long before the secretary or operator on the other end, on the assumption that most people will hang up if no one answers right away.

As we saw in the previous chapter, manufacturing oligopolies and conglomerates attract managers who are money and marketing specialists and who have little direct interest or pride in their products. The same conditions in service-and-information-producing agencies and firms attract managers who have little direct interest or pride in their services. Some managers deliberately adopt policies which make it as difficult as possible for customers to obtain revisions of erroneous computer-printed bills, and which assume that the customers are always guilty until they prove themselves innocent. Others apparently feel that they have more to gain by strong-arming complaints and automatically sending out threatening forms than by reading the customers' letters or acting on their phone calls. Some companies mail bills on a schedule which virtually assures them the customer will incur a late charge every month.

The computer as it has been employed, thus far at least, has shown itself to be the most effective instrument for bureaucratizing interpersonal relations ever invented. As the new microchip technology facilitates the spread of computer-mediated disservices from larger to smaller organizations, the texture of daily life in the U.S. can be expected to grow progressively more formal and impersonal, as well as inefficient. In former times it took dozens of clerks, secretaries and administrators to create a bureaucratic milieu capable of diffusing responsibility for misinformation and disservices. Today thanks to desk-top information processors, small firms and agencies down to the neighborhood hardware store are finding it possible to emulate the bureaucratic style by blaming their disservices on their computer. As a result, bureaucratic modes of behavior and thought may soon become as much a part of everyday American life as apple pie. Let me give a personal example. When I recently sought to settle a bill at a small general hospital, the cashier informed me that the amount due for one week exclusive of doctors' fees was $13,000. Since the patient had been treated for relatively minor injuries which did not require surgery, the account was obviously in error. In fact, as it later turned out, there was an overcharge of $10,000! But the cashier did not know and displayed no interest in finding out why the bill had mounted so rapidly. She never asked what was wrong with the patient. Instead, she returned at once to the computer console and announced with an air of finality: "That's what it says. How do you want to pay or would you like to talk to our financial counselor?"

The fact that the quality of goods and services has been deteriorating despite great advances in industrial technology may seem hard to believe. Countless commercials insist that the new products and services are better than the old. Everything has been done in the name of convenience and efficiency. Until recently, Americans felt that it was un-American to complain and management exploited this lingering bit of puritan sentiment by labeling dissatisfied customers and clients "troublemakers." But I think there is one infallible sign which shows that what has been done in the name of convenience and efficiency has not been achieving its desired effect. And that is the sign of the shrinking dollar. If economies of scale and automation have been making the production of goods and services more efficient, why is it that the general cost of goods and services as measured by the purchasing power of the dollar has risen rather than fallen?

4

Why the Dollar Shrank

Machines used in manufacture, mining, agriculture, and transportation grew larger, more powerful, more automated. Metals grew lighter and stronger. There were synthetic yarns that revolutionized the fabric and apparel industries; plastics that revolutionized the container, furniture, and houseware industries; jet engines that revolutionized air transport; high-yield varieties of seeds, chemical fertilizers, and pesticides that revolutionized agriculture. Everywhere the ingenuity of science and engineering brought forth rivers of labor-saving inventions ranging from automatic high-speed elevators to electric typewriters and automatic car washes. Yet in the midst of the most astonishing period of technological progress in the history of the human species, luxuriating in the possession of countless labor-saving devices that other generations had been able only to dream about, America found itself in the grips of its worst peacetime inflation. Somehow, instead of all that technological progress making goods and services cheaper, by 1980 prices had risen three times higher than their average at the end of World War II.

The current inflation has no precedent in American history.

Throughout the nineteenth century, prices tended to move downward except for brief boom-and-bust phases of the business cycle. Hitherto there have been no sharp, prolonged increases in the cost of living except during wartime. All previous sustained increases in the cost of living have been the clear result of huge government debts contracted during wartime emergencies. After each such emergency, prices have plunged back to their prewar levels. For example, after the Civil War wholesale prices fell 60 percent by 1890 and finished out the century well below what they were in 1800. Similarly, prices fell by almost 50 percent in the aftermath of World War I. But after World War II and the Korean War, prices failed to drop back anywhere near their prewar levels. When the Vietnam War started, prices were already high above those of 1951 and when it was over, the cost of living not only failed to go back to what it had been in 1965, but it started to go up at a faster rate than ever.

Of course the public is convinced that it was the Arab oil embargo that pushed the inflation rate into double digits during the 1970s. But few economists see the increase in petroleum prices as contributing more than a one percent rise in the inflation rate. Even if the cost of energy had gone up merely at the same rate as other goods and services, the inflation rate would still have been close to 10 percent per year in 1980.

The unprecedented new form of inflation that is rampant in the United States today is a symptom of a crisis—a warning buzzer on a vast social machine whose parts are grinding against each other, whose controls have jammed, and whose engine is racing faster and faster but turning out more heat and smoke rather than useful products. To understand why this great machine has begun to function so poorly and why the cost of living has gone up rather then down, we must put ourselves back into the 1930s when the die was cast for the rise of public and private oligopolies, bureaucracies, and the service-and-information economy.

Between 1929 and 1932 more than a quarter of the people in

61

the labor force lost their jobs, nine thousand banks shut their doors, and industrial production fell by half. Fear that a replay of this terrifying experience would lead either to communism or fascism forced the federal government to assume responsibility for regulating the business cycle. This was to be done by following the theories of the British economist John M. Keynes. Downturns in the cycle were to be controlled by increasing the money supply, by lowering interest rates, and by increasing the level of government expenditures, in various combinations as needed. Once business started to pick up again, these measures were to be reversed. There was never any secret that if the stimulants were maintained after business had recovered, the result would be inflation.

We can now see in retrospect that Keynes's theories had a major flaw. Keynes assumed that the government's antirecession stimulants could be turned off as easily as they could be turned on. This proved to be impossible. Superimposed on the short-run ups and downs of the business cycle was a long-range trend that made it politically unacceptable for either major party to restore government agencies and programs to prerecession levels of funding. This long-range trend was the shrinking ability of the agricultural, mining, and manufacturing sectors of the economy to provide employment for everyone who wanted to work. As automation and industrialization replaced workers with machines, measures aimed at stimulating the economy in order to maintain full employment could not be slackened; moreover, government's own role as direct or indirect provider of jobs, grants, pensions, and welfare could not be cut back. As a result, each of the five or six recessions that occurred after 1945 left a legacy which made the task of combating inflation progressively more difficult from a political and humanitarian viewpoint. No administration, Republican or Democratic, was willing or able to let any recession deepen sufficiently to force even a modest drop in prices (as distinguished from a modest drop in the *rate* at which prices were going up). As each recession deepened, the fall in prices

62

predicted by classical economic theory lagged behind the increase in the rate of unemployment. Joblessness increased first, spreading hardship and anxiety among millions of voters. Hence the political costs of recession quickly became too great to follow Keynes's game plan. And so the economic stimulants—lower interest rates, lower taxes, budget deficits, and bigger appropriations for government jobs and subsidies —were administered full strength before prices could return to their prerecession levels. As a result, each successive postwar business upswing started from a higher level of prices, and each successive downswing açcomplished progressively less toward preventing inflation.

Economists now say that to bring the inflation rate down to 2 or 3 percent, a recession would have to be prolonged until the unemployment rate reaches 15 or 20 percent. Unemployment on so massive a scale would bring the economy within range of the dreaded Great Depression, which of course is what all the economic wizardry since World War II has been aimed at preventing. The cost of preventing Great Depression II has been Great Inflation I.

For reasons just mentioned, the number of people gaining all or part of their subsistence from the redistribution of tax money has increased year by year since World War II. By 1980 annual government outlays on the federal, state, and local levels amounted to about 40 percent of the gross national product, and an astonishingly large proportion of American men, women, and children—at least one-third and some would say one-half—now receive all or most of their income from government jobs, Social Security, pensions, and welfare payments. Including jobs, welfare, and transfer payments, the U.S. government is the second largest multinational oligopoly in the world (second to the Soviet Union). How has this contributed to the shrinking of the dollar?

Economists explain that the growth of the government sector has had an inflationary effect on the economy primarily because it has been financed by borrowed funds rather than by current tax receipts. Borrowing by government agencies is the equivalent of putting more money into circulation. Since this additional money does not immediately (if ever) result in putting more goods and services up for sale, government borrowing increases the money supply relative to the amount of goods and services that can be bought. According to classical economic theory, the more money in circulation relative to the amount of goods and services for sale, the less each dollar can buy, that is, the less each dollar is worth—which is what one means by inflation. Between 1960 and 1980 the federal government failed to balance its budget nineteen out of twenty times and piled up a deficit of 435 billion dollars, 85 percent of which was accumulated during the 1970s. Total government debts on the federal, state, and local levels now total over one and a quarter trillion dollars.

Despite these huge numbers, economists affirm that government debt is sufficient to account for only a small part of the rise in the cost of living since World War II. For while government debt has tripled since 1950, the amount owed actually represents a declining portion of the annual gross national product which is worth close to two and a half trillion dollars. The economy has grown so huge that a deficit of twenty billion dollars, for example, probably increases the inflation rate by less than half a percent.

In my view, big government causes inflation not primarily by running up big debts, but by being increasingly wasteful and inefficient. Big government has no demonstrable economies of scale. Lacking the competitive discipline of organizations that must sell in the market, government bureaus and agencies, as they grow larger, typically take more of the taxpayers' money and give less in return. One reason for this is that the heads of government agencies must engage in a constant struggle to prove that they need more money to carry out their mission. If they fail to show that their services are in high demand, their annual share of the budget may be reduced. The classic way to prove that there is a great demand for an agency's services is to show that there is a backlog of potential clients. But in the absence of a competitive market for government services, it is very difficult if not impossible to distinguish between backlogs engendered as a result of an agency being understaffed and efficient, or overstaffed and inefficient. The Postal Service, for example, claims that it is efficient but overworked; its critics claim that it is inefficient and underworked. Without rival delivery services, it is impossible to tell who is right. The Federal Civil Service has eighteen grades of workers with the highest grades earning the most money. According to the government's own General Accounting Office, as many as 40 percent of civil-service jobs are "overclassified"—that is, they could be performed just as well for less money. It is difficult to escape the conclusion that an increasing portion of the allocations for the expansion of government agencies actually constitutes a reward for waste and inefficiency as agencies grow larger and larger.

Moreover, as the number of levels of administrators, supervisors, functionaries, typists, clerks, receptionists, and consultants expands, rigid, depersonalized rules and regulations become ends in themselves. This produces a hardening of the nation's bureaucratic arteries and stupefying orgies of paper and tape work. The Federal Paper Work Commission estimates that it costs the Federal Government one billion dollars to print forms, another billion to provide instructions, and another 1.7 billion to file and store the replies. It costs the business community about 30 billion dollars to fill out the forms. Incidentally, when the House of Representatives was looking for ways to reduce this burden it produced a seven-volume, 2,285-page report.

Is there any wonder that the dollar is shrinking? If taxes rise faster than the quality of government services, then the taxpayers get less for their money—and that is inflation.

Everybody pays more for less when waste and inefficiency in government bureaus increase. As red tape, paper shuffling, form-filling, passing the buck, runarounds, and interagency jurisdictional disputes keep getting worse, the dollar shrinks. The dollar shrinks still more when businesses and consumers must pay for substitute or supplementary services on top of what they have paid for with their taxes. If the public schools deteriorate, people pay more for tutors and private instruction; if police protection deteriorates, everybody pays more for locks, alarms, and private guards; if the roads and streets deteriorate, there is more to pay for auto repairs and alternative modes of transportation; if the Post Office can't deliver a letter or package, the country not only pays tax money on top of stamps to make up the postal deficit, but it pays for extra telephone calls and for private delivery services. Businesses try to meet these extra costs by raising prices. Consumers try to meet these extra costs by demanding wage increases, which in turn get passed back to everybody in the form of additional price hikes.

Two British economists, Robert Bacon and Walter Eltis, have proposed that even if there is no deterioration in the quality of services nor any deficit financing, expansion of the public sector will lead to inflation. Taxpayers, they argue, tend to disregard public services in thinking about their standard of living. People don't see the connection between their taxes and the social benefits provided by the government; instead they see their taxes as a personal loss which they then strive to overcome by demanding higher wages. Obviously this theory applies more forcefully if the services rendered are deteriorating at the same time that taxpayers have to pay more for them.

What about the effect of the proliferation of governmental agencies concerned with the environment, health, and safety? Clearly the growth of regulatory agencies adds to the amount of red tape, paper-shuffling, and form-filling, and these bureaucratic measures must be included among the sources of inflation on the government side. Goodyear Tire & Rubber Company, for example, estimates that it spent 35.5 million dollars and 34 employee-years filling out forms and writing reports for six government agencies in 1979. But in other re-spects, the inflationary impact of the regulations themselves may be quite small. Many of the price increases attributable to stepped-up government regulations for clean air and water, for the disposal of toxic chemicals, for safer drugs and more wholesome foods, and for protection against occupational haz-ards actually are not so much price increases as shifts in pay-ments from one set of commodities and services to another set of commodities and services. Knowingly or not, the public has always paid for the reckless and incompetent discharge of in-dustrial effluents into the air and water and for the dumping of toxic wastes. But the payments were not included in the price of the pollution-causing products or services. Rather they were included in the price of other products and services which were needed to compensate for the effects of pollution on people and their possessions. Take air pollution. Its pre-vention will cost billions in the form of auto exhaust devices and factory chimney scrubbers. But its existence has already cost billions in the form of extra coats of paint, crumbling masonry, and clogged air filters, not to mention huge medical and insurance bills for damaged lungs and hearts. Similar rea-soning applies to auto safety, occupational hazards, and food and drug standards where the costs in terms of the loss of "human capital"—what the injured and deceased would have earned if their health had not been impaired or they had not died prematurely—run very high. Until economists render a more accurate accounting of the hidden costs of the absence of regulations, one should be extremely wary of the claims that reducing pollution and promoting health and safety are in themselves inflationary. What shrinks the dollar is not that one pays more, but that one pays more for less.

I should note that not all economists agree that the growth of the government sector of capitalist economies necessarily leads to bureaucratic "diseconomies" of scale. Some econo-mists even point to the postwar success stories of the Japanese and German economies as evidence of the need for more rather than less big government. The rate of growth of industrial productivity in West Germany from 1972 to 1978 was four times greater than in the United States. Yet government absorbs over 50 percent of the West German gross national product. In Japan, where productivity increased five times faster than in the United States during the 1970s, "there is a degree of central investment planning and government control that would make any good capitalist cry." But I think these comparisons may be misleading because of specific historical factors that conditioned the post-World War II industrial growth of each country. For example, neither Japan nor Germany has been burdened with huge military-industrial programs which are notorious for their inflationary wastefulness and cost overruns (as will be seen in a moment). Moreover, many of Japan's and Germany's factories were destroyed in the war, and by starting from scratch they were able to incorporate technological innovations at a faster rate than the United States. Finally, there is a critical difference between the degree of development of service-and-information-producing jobs in the United States compared with Japan or Germany. A large portion of government's share in the United States economy goes to supporting people-processing and information-processing jobs rather than to supporting manufacturing jobs. This is reflected in the fact that the ratio of manufacturing to nonmanufacturing employment in the United States is about 2:1 but only 1:1 in West Germany and 1.4:1 in Japan. America's government is more inflationary than Japan's or Germany's because its principal product is paper and talk.

In the United States, the government sector produces far more services than goods. The opposite is true in Japan and Germany where government is part-owner or indirect partner of the major manufacturing corporations. The products of these companies must compete with the products of private companies and hence there is a greater check on waste and inefficiency than there is in an agency like the U.S. Postal Service or the U.S. Department of Defense. Moreover, to make the United States situation still less comparable with that of Japan and Germany, to the extent that the U.S. government is a direct or indirect partner in the production of goods rather than services, the items produced are mainly military equipment and hardware for which special provisions are made to reward the manufacturers no matter how inefficient and wasteful they may be.

In assessing the contribution U.S. government spending makes to inflation, the defense budget certainly merits special attention. In addition to the bureaucratic inefficiencies and sheer waste inherent in any agency charged with the task of spending one hundred and fifty billion dollars a year, the Department of Defense awards contracts for military equipment on a cost-plus basis. This guarantees the megacorporations with which the Pentagon deals a steady rate of profit regardless of how much their actual costs of production exceed estimates made at contract signing. With their profits assured, these companies have little incentive to eliminate waste and inefficiency and the taxpayers again find themselves spending more to get less.

At least one industrial engineer, Seymour Melman, has long argued that the inflationary effects of military spending are not confined to firms that hold military contracts. The effects spill over into the entire private sector by creating a pool of executives and engineers who have no experience with meeting production deadlines and staying within budget allocations and who are all too prone to make up for their time and cost overruns by raising prices. Their sloppiness fits in well with the ability of oligopoly conglomerates in the private sector to set administered prices. And this brings us to the role of the private sector of the economy in the inflationary process.

Up to now, I have been discussing the inflationary role of big government, specifically the inflationary effects of the failure to reverse the antidepression stimulants advocated by Keynes, the explosive growth of deficit financing, and the waste and inefficiency inherent in the production of government services and armaments by bureaucracies that are not subject to the discipline that comes from selling products in a competitive market. But the shrinking dollar cannot be blamed on big government alone. Big business is also a mighty engine of inflation, and I think that it is impossible to say whether it is the private or public sector that is more to blame for pushing up prices since World War II.

It is the formation of giant oligopoly corporations that lies at the heart of the private sector's contribution to the shrinking of the dollar. With a handful of companies dominating major industries, the U.S. government is not the only producer of goods and services that is in a position to avoid the disciplinary effects of a competitive marketplace. Where oligopoly reigns, prices no longer reflect competition among a large number of independent firms, each striving to undersell the rest. Instead, by tacit agreement among industry leaders, prices reflect decisions made by managers to achieve a targeted profit. (This does not mean that all competition ceases but that it shifts from an emphasis on price to other factors such as packaging, advertising, and salesmanship.)

Consumers pay these "administered prices" because they regard the products as essential to their way of life and know of no other means of acquiring them. While there may be smaller firms that produce a comparable product, such firms are unlikely to win a substantial share of the market by engaging in price competition with the industry leaders. To make inroads against the oligopolies, a small firm will need to keep its prices down while spending large sums on advertising to acquaint customers with its products. If by some prodigious feat of entrepreneurship a small firm does get to the point of threatening the industry leaders, a coup de grâce will soon be delivered. It will be bought up by the larger firms.

Administered prices are the civilian counterparts of military cost-plus contracts. They sap management's determination to resist wage demands. Secure in the knowledge that wage hikes can be passed on to consumers, management allows inflationary wage settlements to be built into the collective bargaining process; this has culminated in some form of the indexing of wages to prices in most labor contracts negotiated during the 1970s.

The ability of oligopoly conglomerates to administer prices also goes a long way toward explaining the appearance of the mystifying phenomenon known as stagflation. Theoretically, in a free market economy, as inventories accumulate during a recession and production is cut back, prices ought to decline at least as fast as people lose their jobs. But when, as we have seen, the top five hundred concerns own 72 percent of all assets used in manufacturing, the degree of concentration in the private sector is so great that leading companies find they could remain profitable, or at least cut their losses, by increasing prices even in the midst of recessions. The classic instance of this expression of oligopoly power is the rise in the price of gasoline despite a substantial drop in consumer demand, but many other industries—notably chemicals, autos, and steel—have been doing the same thing.

Administered prices also have an inflationary impact through their effect on the pattern of corporate borrowing. According to the Keynesian game plan, inflation was to have been brought under control by raising the cost of loans to corporations whenever the economy tended to "overheat." But if they can pass along the added cost of borrowing money to the consumer, corporations can keep on borrowing even in the face of higher interest rates. By relying on administered prices to overcome high interest rates, U.S. corporations, just like the U.S. government, have gradually increased their dependence on deficit financing to supply their need for capital. In the past U.S. corporations obtained money for operating expenses and expansion primarily by plowing back income generated from sales, by selling stock in the company, and to a lesser extent by borrowing. But since 1950 the private sector has relied less on internal funds and stock issues—which are not debts—and more on bonds, mortgages, and bank loans, which are debts. As socialist leader Michael Harrington has pointed out, the lack of awareness about the growth of corporate debt contrasts with the public's awareness of government debt. "Corporations—whose executives delight in lecturing the nation on fiscal responsibility—are much more deeply involved in deficit financing than the government." Public debt as a percentage of gross national product has declined since 1950, but private debt as a percentage of gross national product has more than doubled. Corporate debt has gone up fourteen times while the debt of the federal government has gone up only three times. Of course, borrowing itself is not necessarily inflationary. The trouble arises when as a result of falling productivity, firms cannot pay off their loans out of income and have to borrow some more to pay back what they have already borrowed.

The more money a company owes, the less cash it has on hand, the more it must borrow to preserve its cash flow, the faster the rate at which it must borrow, the more it costs to borrow, the more it tries to preserve its "liquidity" by raising its prices. The proof that this is what has been happening can be found in the fact that not only have U.S. corporations gone steadily deeper into hock, but their debts have steadily shifted from long-term obligations such as bonds to short-term bank loans and commercial I.O.U.s. In the 1950s internal funds generated each year were sufficient to pay off these short-term debts. Now the short-term corporate debt total is twice as big as the nonfinancial corporate sector's annual disposable income. In the early 1950s corporations had on hand eight dollars for every ten dollars in short-term debt. In the mid-1970s they had only two dollars in cash for every ten dollars of short-term debt. To meet these short-term obligations and the interest on them, U.S. corporations now must keep borrowing at an accelerating rate. This raises the cost of money but it does not slow down the rate of borrowing, because again oligopolies, with their power to administer prices, keep passing on the extra costs to the consumer.

Now we can better appreciate why the new breed of executives who have presided over the debauchery of the "Made in U.S.A." label are under so much pressure to turn a fast buck. As companies come to depend more on short-term financing, cash flow becomes the lifeblood of the firm. Premium rewards go to executives who are adept at meeting short-term obligations rather than to those who want to lay the basis for sound profitability in the years ahead. The natural selection of inflation, so to speak, selects for inflation-adapted administrative personalities.

Corporation executives are not alone in being subject to the psychological restraints and compulsions of the Great Inflation. As the dollar goes on shrinking year after year, a similar type of selection takes place throughout the entire society. Government officials plan on balancing their budgets from the extra revenues to be obtained when taxpayers move up into inflated tax brackets; Social Security checks and union wage settlements get pegged to the cost of living index; consumers increase their home mortgages and personal loans in expectation of being able to liquidate their debts out of inflated incomes. By the same token, people lose faith in their savings accounts and their pensions and search desperately for investments that will keep their money from shrinking. All of this adds to the rate of inflation. Like the feedback on a squealing loudspeaker, or the stampede of a herd of cattle, the selection for inflation-adapted psychological ways of thinking and feeling is in itself a source of inflation. But in acknowledging the importance of America's "inflationary psychology," we must not fall into the trap of supposing that inflation is primarily a "state of mind." It is a state of inefficiency.

To sum up, the U.S. dollar has shrunk for essentially the same reason that the United States has had an epidemic of shoddy goods and catastrophic disservices. Since World War II, despite all the technological wonders aimed at saving labor and raising output per worker, something else has been lowering output and wasting labor at an even faster rate. And this something else is the fundamental change that has occurred in the organization and nature of work in the United States. I mean the shift from a goods-producing to a service-and-information-producing labor force and the rise of giant government and corporate bureaucracies and oligopolies filled with alienated managers and employees. The effect of this shift has been to decrease the efficiency of the entire production system and to give people less for their money.

Official figures show that the productivity of the American economy—the value of goods and services produced divided by the number of workers—has risen at a slower and slower rate since the end of World War II. Nonfarm business productivity rose at 3.4 percent per year from 1948 to 1955, at 3.1 percent between 1955 and 1965, at 2.3 percent between 1965 and 1973, and at only one percent between 1973 and 1980.

Ominous as these figures are, they scarcely tell the whole story of the declining efficiency of the U.S. economy. They still show that productivity has been going up rather than down since World War II. The problem is that when economists measure productivity, they make absolutely no provision for the quality of what is produced. If five million new toasters, vacuum cleaners, and sewing machines break down each year, the cost of repairing them is not subtracted from the dollar value of the manufacturing sector; rather it gets added to the output of the service sector. Ditto when two million cars are recalled for hazardous defects.

As we saw in the discussion of product quality, no one has the slightest idea how much product "down time" costs the American consumer. We also saw that there is virtually a complete blank as far as product life-history data are concerned. The dearth of standardized product-quality information—information about how long things last and how often they break down—which is in itself a symptom of the whole product-quality problem, raises doubts about the meaning of the standard productivity indices as well as about the meaning of the inflation rate.

The measurement problem is even more acute in the information- and people-processing sectors. Economists know only how to measure services; they cannot measure disservices and misinformation. If a surgeon removes the wrong organ and the patient expires, the surgeon's fee gets added to the output of the medical profession and the funeral costs get added to the output of the undertakers and gravediggers. The cost of delivering midnight-blue sofas with sky-blue love seats that have holes in them is a plus for the trucking industry. The money spent on phone calls trying to correct billing errors is a plus for the telephone company. Nowhere in the economists' account books is there a tally for the anger and frustration of the man who has lost his credit rating for seven years because a bored clerk in a video terminal cockpit typed in the wrong Social Security number.

The growth of the service-and-information economy and of giant government and corporate oligopolies and bureaucracies has had a far more pervasive effect on American life than most people realize. As we shall see in the next chapter, there are consequences that are being felt even in the privacy of America's bedrooms. For the rise of our inflationary, oligopolized and bureaucratized service-and-information economy has drastically altered the sexual composition of the labor force. And I think I can show that this change in turn is primarily responsible for the sudden growth of new forms of sexuality and marriage found in America today.

5

Why
Women
Left
Home

"Miss America Sells It." It was September 1969 and they were out to zap the "degrading, mindless boob-girlie" sexism of the Atlantic City beauty pageant. Dumping padded bras, girdles, false eyelashes, copies of *Playboy,* and steno pads into a "freedom trashcan," they placed a Miss America crown on the head of a live sheep and sang:

Ain't she sweet
Making profit off her meat.

Later that year members of Women's International Terrorist Conspiracy from Hell (WITCH for short) disrupted a fashion show for brides by singing (to the tune of the wedding march):

Here come the slaves,
Off to their graves.

In August of the following year as ten thousand feminists marched along Fifth Avenue, Kate Millett declared: "Today is the beginning of a new movement. Today is the end of millenniums of oppression." Heckled by bystanders who called them bra-less "traitors," a thousand women marched in Boston and two thousand in San Francisco. In Miami women smashed crockery at a "liberation garden party" while in Philadelphia's Rittenhouse Square feminists prepared themselves for the struggle by taking free open-air karate lessons. Meanwhile, back in New York's Duffy Square, Mary Orovan was making the sign of the cross at a ceremony honoring Susan B. Anthony, intoning: "In the name of the Mother, the Daughter, and the Holy Granddaughter. Ah-Women. Ah-Women," while the crowd flaunted placards reading: "Repent, Male Chauvinists, Your World Is Coming To An End" and "Don't Cook Dinner Tonight—Starve A Rat." Suddenly women were on the rampage. Almost overnight, from coast to coast, books, journals, magazines, college courses, talk shows, and the President of the United States heralded the dawn of a new feminist order.

Timing is crucial. Why, in the words of historian Carl Degler, did "a renewed feminist movement fairly burst upon the nation in the 1960's?" One theory is that the feminist vanguard got its training in the civil rights campaigns and in the anti-Vietnam war protests. Women "learned to respect themselves and to know their own strength" but "they were simultaneously thrust into subservient roles—as secretary, sex object, housekeeper, 'dumb chick.' " They then realized that they would be oppressed even by men in the radical left antiwar groups, and this supposedly triggered the formation of the first militant organizations in 1967, which proliferated "throughout the year and into 1968 at an astounding rate."

But what has to be explained is why this feminist vanguard suddenly found themselves leading millions of women who had never participated in the antiwar or civil rights movements, including many women who were embarrassed by the bra-shedding and the man-baiting aspects of feminism.

The popular rebellion-by-inspiration theory gives insufficient consideration to changes that were taking place in the basic structure of American economic and political life—changes which made certain rebellious actions seem necessary to a cross section of American women and which at the same time prevented society from suppressing the activists.

Not every kind of rebellious action by an aggrieved minority attracted support or was found to be irrepressible during the 1960s. Armies of atheists, for example, did not suddenly turn up to picket Sunday church services; and it was not for lack of trying that communists and socialists were unable to stir American workers into expropriating the means of production from their bosses. I think we need to do more than simply connect the rebellious outbursts of the sixties one to another in a chronological series from civil rights to antiwar, to women's liberation, to gay liberation, in order to understand why so much that is new and strange suddenly took hold in America. This kind of reasoning inevitably leads to a chain of previous incidents that has no knowable beginning. Also, the links appear to be logically arbitrary. Why couldn't gay liberation or women's liberation have come before the civil rights movement? No doubt some of these liberationist and "counter-culture" movements inspired each other. No doubt some leaders of one were schooled in another; and no doubt specific calls for black power, or women power, or gay power were echoes of strategies and tactics passed along from movement to movement. But none of this is to say that the last was dependent on the first in the sense that without the civil rights activists there would have been no antiwar movement, no women's liberation, and no gay liberation. That all these movements were bunched together merely confirms the existence of a pervasive and radical cultural upheaval. If we want to understand the reasons for this upheaval, must we not turn to deeper and more basic changes in American society?

Another unsatisfactory notion is that the rebellion came when it did because it was the result of a long slow buildup.

"The rebellion took over 200 years to foment" writes one feminist, presumably because two centuries were needed to develop the sense of common purpose and the necessary leadership. The problem with this idea is that in the two decades immediately preceding the rebellion, organized feminist activity was shrinking, not growing. In fact, after World War II, feminism was almost nonexistent compared to earlier decades when the struggle for women's suffrage was still going on. People who grew up during the 1940s and 1950s remember them as decades of declining enthusiasm for the feminist cause. If anything, were these not antifeminist years? Not only was feminism attacked in popular books such as *Modern Women: The Lost Sex* by Ferdinand Lundberg and Marynia Farnham, but motherhood and marriage were as fashionable as white Cadillacs with fins and three-martini lunches. Many feminist leaders recount their personal struggle against the mass media's attempt to glamorize housewives and homebody husband-pleasers in the postwar years. Betty Friedan felt it was a time when women were expected to put on eye makeup in order to run the vacuum cleaner. Others recall that doctors feared that working mothers would harm their children and their husbands. Psychiatrists diagnosed women careerists who competed with men as suffering from "penis envy." Anthropologist Ashley Montagu warned: "I put it down as an axiom that no woman with a husband and small children can hold a full-time job and be a good homemaker at one and the same time."

Apparently, women agreed. A Gallup poll in 1936 reported that three-quarters of women disapproved of married women taking jobs, and a *Fortune* magazine poll in 1946 showed that more women than men expressed misgivings about placing careers before families. One early researcher found that nonearner housewives in the late 1950s resented and derided their earner counterparts and that these women themselves shared the low esteem of the stay-at-homes. At that time the wife who held a job, no less than the housewife, believed that women with jobs were nervous, unloving, inferior mates, and inefficient housekeepers.

I think that the most compelling evidence that feminism was losing rather than gaining strength prior to the rebellion was the rise in the birthrate. During the 1940s and 1950s the whole country went on an extraordinary procreative binge, commonly known as the post-World War II "baby boom." When women like Betty Friedan protested against too much motherhood in their lives, they were not talking about a figment of imagination; they were talking about an extraordinary bumper crop of babies that they themselves had just produced.

So one cannot explain the timing of the rebellion in terms of a steady growth of feminist strength. Rather we have to explain why antifeminism abruptly gave rise to its opposite.

The baby boom and the "baby bust" that followed it provide an important clue for understanding this abrupt turnabout. The clue is this: the birthrate peaked in 1957, a full decade before the feminist outburst. So the feminist rebellion could not have caused the "baby bust," yet whatever caused the "baby bust" might have caused the feminist rebellion. But in order to follow out this clue, we shall have to delve somewhat into the question of why birthrates rise or fall.

Baby booms and busts have not come and gone like business booms and busts. Throughout almost two hundred years of census-taking from 1800 to the present, there was never a decade until 1940–1950 when the birthrate rose by even a small percentage. Decade after decade it had moved monotonously downward. Then between 1940 and 1949 it zoomed up 35 percent. And from 1950 to 1957 it went up by another 15 percent, rising a record seven years in a row to peak at a level last seen forty years earlier. The first World War and the "roaring twenties" had been completely different; between 1920 and 1930, despite years of economic boom, the birthrate kept on its historic downward course, dropping every year but one for a total decline of 25 percent.

What lay behind the persistent decline in the U.S. birthrate?

Despite some recent criticism, the best explanation continues to be that the decline was caused by the change from a rural, farming way of life to an urban, industrial way of life. Much comparative evidence indicates that urban-industrial development caused birthrates to fall because it changed the balance of economic costs and benefits involved in rearing children. To put it bluntly, children in industrialized cities tend to cost more and to be economically less valuable to their parents than children on farms. City families with large numbers of children get dragged down in the competition for economic improvement whereas farm families with large numbers of children tend to get ahead.

In predominantly rural America of colonial times and the early 1800s, children had been an economic blessing. They cost relatively little to bring up because much of their food, shelter, and clothing was produced on the family farm. At the same time they contributed to their own upkeep by starting to do valuable chores while they were still very young. Finally, as farm parents grew old and feeble, it was relatively easy for their children to pay them back by taking care of them.

The economic balance in urban and industrial settings is different. City children are more likely to be an economic curse than a blessing. On the cost side, all food, clothing, and shelter has to be purchased. Furthermore, in order for city children to make a substantial contribution to household income they have to go to school. The more schooling, the greater the potential return for both parents and child, but the greater the risk and expense. This means that on the benefit side, urban parents cannot expect even a modest return on their "investment" until middle age. Meanwhile, the expense of getting old and sick was steadily increasing, partly because parents could expect to live longer as a result of desirable but costly medical intervention. By the mid-twentieth century the costs of old age could no longer be met even by relatively affluent children, and the burden of providing for aged and infirm people passed almost entirely from the family to the

Social Security Administration, private medical insurance, pension funds, and assorted welfare programs where it remains today. When that happened, the bottom line for the costs and benefits of rearing children showed a lifetime deficit, a deficit that has become increasingly severe.

There is another way the combination of urbanization and industrialization brings about declining birthrates and that is by improving the general health of a population, especially of infants and children. As health conditions improve and infant mortality falls—the long-term historic trend in the United States—parents can achieve a favorable cost/benefit ratio by means of fewer births. This factor accelerates the trends caused by increasingly unfavorable cost/benefits characteristic of large families. In other words other things being equal, the U.S. birthrate would not have dropped so fast or so low had the health conditions in Chicago or New York been as bad as those in Cairo or Calcutta (which partially accounts for the fact that the birthrate still remains so high in big cities in the developing countries).

Industrialization did not create every feature of the contemporary American family. For example, we know that most Americans in George Washington's time did not have grandparents or uncles or aunts living with them as so many textbooks still erroneously report. It was usually a "nuclear family" then just as it is today. Researchers have also recently shown that most American families were always relatively small. The *average* number of children per family today is only about one less than in 1850. But the relative proportion of families with small and large numbers of children has changed considerably. In 1850 there were seven times as many families with four or more children as today. As for families with no children present, there are four times more today than in 1850. So the main effect of the declining birthrate was a gradual disappearance of families with large numbers of children and a steady increase in the proportion of families with no children at all (trends that are not adequately expressed if one considers only changes in the *average* size of families). These are the most important changes in the family brought about by industrialization and urbanization.

Does this mean that parents want children only for selfish economic reasons? Of course not. Parents value children for noneconomic motives, especially the joys of mutual love and affection. Many see reproduction as a form of immortality; others see it as a religious or patriotic duty. Families are not businesses whose only interest in having children is to turn a profit. But the economics of child-rearing always modify these other motivations. When a couple says, "We cannot afford another child," that does not mean that their only interest in having children is to enjoy a lifetime favorable balance of economic benefits. By the same token, the fact that a couple refrains from openly discussing the economic costs and benefits of child-rearing does not mean that they are uninfluenced by such considerations.

What then caused the baby boom? Although the long-range trend in the balance of costs and benefits for getting married and having children was increasingly negative, immediately after World War II there was a temporary reversal of this trend. Suddenly more young people could afford to get married and have children. First of all, the United States emerged from World War II as the number-one global superpower. As America's corporations gained control over vast new markets and new sources of cheap energy and raw materials, the economy expanded rapidly leading to relatively high levels of employment and stable prices. At the same time, as a reward for military service, the U.S. government decided to bestow an unprecedented series of benefits on its returning veterans. Fourteen million ex-members of the armed forces—mostly young unmarried men—became eligible for substantial severance bonuses, cheap life insurance, guaranteed low-cost mortgages, and tuition and monthly stipends for education with dependency allotments. In effect, these programs temporarily shifted a considerable portion of the actual and anticipated costs of getting married and of rearing children from the nuclear family to the federal budget. Although not consciously designed as such, this shift, especially as it reduced the cost of housing, really amounted to a subsidy worth several thousands of dollars for each procreative couple. As a result, between 1940 and 1960 the number of single women aged twenty to twenty-nine years dropped from 36 percent to 20 percent while the birthrate rose from eighty to one hundred twenty live births per thousand women. By the time women born in 1908 had reached fifty years of age (in 1958) only half of them had given birth to two or more children. But by the time women born in 1927—the baby-boom mothers—had reached thirty-five years of age, three-quarters of them had already had two or more children.

This rush to marital bliss and parenthood proves that until the 1960s America was still a profoundly pro-natalist society, despite all the previous years of declining birthrates. The traditional *marital and procreative imperative* was still very much alive. According to this imperative, sex was supposed to be confined to marriage, everyone ideally had to get married, and every marriage was supposed to lead to reproduction. The function of marriage cum natural sex in other words was to promote reproduction and child-rearing as the primary duty and responsibility of anyone, male or female, who wanted to experience sexual pleasure. A popular nineteenth-century marriage guide had put it this way:

> When, but only when mankind properly LOVE and MARRY and then rightly generate, CARRY, NURSE and EDUCATE their children, they will be in deed and in truth the holy and happy sons and daughters of the "Lord Almighty," compared with those miserable and depraved scapegoats of humanity which infest our earth.

Of course these ideals were never universally, nor perhaps even usually, obeyed, not even during the nineteenth century. We know from the warnings of doctors, preachers, politicians, and educators that masturbation, prostitution, and other kinds of "unnatural" sex flourished both in and out of the bonds of wedlock. We also know that men and women were making increasing use of contraceptive devices, that men refrained from getting married until they could support a wife, and that couples refrained from having children until they could afford them. While there is no way we can reliably estimate the absolute degree of noncompliance with the marital and procreative imperative, the steadily falling birthrate suggests that the gap between values and behavior increased during the nineteenth and early twentieth centuries.

Toward the end of the nineteenth century, as the cost/benefits of marriage and procreation deteriorated and as the birthrate declined, the federal government and the states passed harsh new laws which banned the teaching of birth control techniques, the manufacture, sale, or use of contraceptive devices, and which prohibited premarital and extramarital sex, or "unnatural" sex by married couples. Within marriage or without, mouth-to-genital or anal sex became subject to criminal prosecution under numerous harsh antisodomy measures. Indulgence in such "unnatural" acts became punishable by life in prison in Georgia, by thirty years in Connecticut, and by twenty years in Florida, Massachusetts, Minnesota, Nebraska, and New York. Similar laws applied to those who sought to circumvent the procreative imperative by the use of animals as sexual partners. Even masturbation came to be a major crime. The Indiana statute, for example, condemned masturbation by a man or a woman of a person under twenty-one as sodomy which was punishable by fourteen years in jail. In New Jersey, masturbation of one partner by another regardless of age or marital status became punishable by three years imprisonment under a statute aimed at "any person who in private is guilty of an act of lewdness or carnal indecency with another." As for the man or woman who turned to solitary and private masturbation, nineteenth- and early twentieth-century medical authorities made their life a living hell by warning them that they would get skin cancer and become imbeciles.

A corollary of the marital and procreative imperatives was

that once women got married, they had to stay home and take care of the children. During the early days of the factory system, England had experimented with the possibility of using married women as workers in factories. It was found that married women would accept lower pay than their husbands, but it also soon became apparent that marriage, procreation, and the family itself were all threatened by that practice. The leaders of the British Parliament feared that if the preference for hiring married women were allowed to run its course, there would soon be an end to the laboring classes since women who worked all day would obviously be unwilling to marry and support unemployable husbands or rear children—at least not the kind of children who were likely to be suitable for employment in an industrializing economy.

All the industrializing nations found that the best way to preserve and increase the quantity and quality of their laboring classes was to prohibit or discourage the employment of married women in factory jobs. In the United States, the temptation to push married women into factory work was never as strong as in Europe because the great current of immigration into the New World provided ample numbers of qualified men, at least until the immigration laws were changed in the 1920s.

Prior to World War II, the marital and procreative imperative and married woman's homebody role suited the government, churches, and employers of labor. Traditionally, the government held that the more people, the bigger the armed forces, the greater the security of life and property. Also, the more people, the greater the tax base, the better equipped the armed forces, and the greater the available wealth for the government bureaucracy. From the industrialist and merchant point of view, the more people, the bigger the market for real estate and goods and the cheaper the supply of labor. Similarly, for organized religion, the more people, the more souls to save and pray for, the higher the level of economic support, and the greater the political influence of each denomination.

Women's homebody role also suited the male breadwinner. Wives who went to work posed a double threat: They undermined the basis of the husband's dominant role in family and society and they drove male wages down by increasing the supply of workers. These incentives explain why the unions were once one of the great bastions of antifeminism: The men who ran the unions wanted women to stay home for the same reason they wanted blacks to stay on the farms and immigrants to stay across the ocean—to force up the price of labor. For unionized men a worker's wage had at least to be "sufficient to keep his wife and children out of competition with himself." In the words of a turn-of-the-century Boston labor union leader: "The demand for female labor is an insidious assault upon the home; it is the knife of the assassin aimed at the family circle."

Throughout most of America's past, therefore, men from all social classes joined forces to keep married women at home where they were unpaid maidservants for their husbands and unpaid baby-makers for everybody else. The employment figures for the beginning of the century bear this out. In 1890 women made up 17 percent of the paid labor force. But the overwhelming majority of these women were single, widowed, or divorced. The typical and preferred pattern was for a married woman never to work for pay. If a girl's family could afford it, she stayed home until she got married. If not, she went to work until she got married and then quit immediately. The typical women workers were girls waiting to get married, "spinsters" unable for one reason or another to get married, women who had been abandoned by their husbands, and widows. In 1890 only 14 percent of the women in the job force were married and these women represented only 5 percent of working-age women. Most of these married working women were blacks and recent immigrants. For a married, native-born white woman to work outside the home for money was a phenomenal rarity: only 2 percent of them did it. In contrast, 23 percent of married adult black women in 1890 already held jobs (and not because they were "liberated" but because they were poor!).

Except for a tiny group of privileged female doctors, lawyers, college teachers, and other professionals, scarcely any native-born married white women went to work unless their husbands died or abandoned them. A woman simply did not get married to a man who could not "support" her, which meant that many women had to postpone getting married and that many remained single for life. Although we think of the present feminist situation as characterized by a new tendency to delay marriage, the record for late marriages was actually achieved in 1900. Over 40 percent of American women that year between the ages of twenty and twenty-nine had never had a husband. But unlike the somewhat smaller group of single women in their twenties today, the unmarried women of the past could not live alone or with male or female age mates; they remained instead with their parents or they moved in with married brothers or sisters, and were frequently looked down upon and humiliated for their lack of success in capturing a breadwinner husband.

Until World War II, therefore, the proportion of *married* women who participated in the workforce remained small. In 1940, despite a sharp increase in working wives during the Great Depression, only 15 percent of married women who had a husband present held an outside job. But this was soon to change. By 1960 the proportion of employed married women with husbands present had risen to 30 percent and by 1980 to about 50 percent. More than half of married women in the prime reproductive age thirty-five years or younger now hold jobs. As one might expect, the proportion of married women who go to work is highest among those who have no small children to take care of at home. This proportion has climbed to a phenomenal 80 percent among married women less than thirty-five years old. But the proportion of young married women who go to work even though (or because) they have small children to take care of is also astonishingly high: 40 percent of those under thirty-five who have one or more children under six; and over 60 percent of those who have a child at home between six and eighteen.

Has this drastic change in the participation rate of married women in the labor force finally broken the back of the marital and procreative imperative? I think so. The traditional pro-natal system could tolerate increased participation by *unmarried women* in the labor force; but it could not survive increased participation by *married women*. The fulfillment of the marital and procreative imperative hinged on women staying home in order to raise children. While one can easily think of alternative arrangements such as day-care centers which might resolve the contradiction between jobs and babies, no such arrangements were or are available on the requisite national scale, primarily because day care has to be paid in cash, while home care was paid with sentiment. As married women poured into the labor force, all the dire warnings that procreation and employment outside the home were incompatible suddenly came true. The baby boom collapsed, and the fertility rate began its historic plunge, reaching zero-population-growth levels in 1972 and falling still further to an average of 1.8 children per woman by 1980. Incidentally, the idea that the baby boom collapsed because of the introduction of the "pill" can easily be dismissed, since the bust began in 1957 while the pill was not released for public use until June 1960. As late as 1964, when fertility was falling with unprecedented speed, only 10 percent of married women of childbearing age were using the "pill."

I think the most misguided notion about the end of the baby boom and the transformation of housewife into wage laborer is the belief that women's liberation made the housewife dissatisfied with her homebody baby-making role and so she went out and found a job. Women's liberation did not *create* the working woman; rather the working woman—especially the working housewife—created women's liberation. As we have just seen, the massive shift of married women into the labor force had already taken place *before* the period of intensive consciousness-raising. In the words of University of Florida anthropologist Maxine Margolis:

Thus, while the past fifteen years have witnessed the entry of women, particularly wives and mothers, into the labor force in unprecedented numbers, popular opinion only belatedly recognized the importance of this phenomenon. While the media devoted much space to "bra burning" and other supposed atrocities of the women's movement, little attention was paid to the reality of women's work which had set the stage for the revival of feminism.

Moreover, it is a great deception to believe that women went out and found jobs. Given the nature of the U.S. economy and its chronically high levels of unemployment, the mere desire to find a job is not enough to land one. The jobs have to be there. Between 1947 and 1978, twenty-five million new jobs were filled by women. And by 1979 two out of every three new jobs were being taken by women. Feminists have often neglected to say that these jobs find the women as much as the women find the jobs. To understand why the feminist rebellion took place precisely when it did, we must understand both sides of the equation: what it was that compelled or enticed married women to want to look for work, and what it was in the national economy that created vast numbers of new jobs that went looking for married women.

On the worker's side, married women's initial motivation was to provide a supplement to their breadwinner-husband's income. The 1950s and early 1960s were a period of consumer expectations aimed at the ownership of clothing, household furnishings, automobiles, telephones, and many new or previously prohibitively expensive product lines such as washing machines, dryers, dishwashers, and color TV sets. Much of married women's initial surge toward the job market was keyed toward purchasing specific products deemed important for a decent standard of living in what was then being called the affluent society. To achieve these limited goals married women were quite willing to accept part-time, temporary, and dead-end jobs.

As all the polls and surveys of the 1950s showed, the baby-

90

boom mothers had no intention of giving up their homebody role. At first, the married women who moved into the labor force were primarily housewives over forty-five whose children had "left the nest." But a decisive break came in the early 1960s when younger married women, with children under eighteen, began to enter the labor force in droves. This break was not caused by a rise in feminine consciousness; rather it was caused by the beginning of the Great Inflation.

By the early 1960s the baby-boom parents were finding it increasingly difficult to achieve or hold on to middle-class standards of consumption for themselves and their children, and the wife's job had begun to play a crucial role in family finances. As the first of the baby-boom children approached college age, the burden of medical care, schooling, clothing, and housing for the average family increased far faster than the male breadwinner's salary.

Official government statistics place the beginning of the inflationary surge after 1965 and indicate that spendable weekly earnings (in constant dollars) of workers with three dependents fell by only about one percent between then and 1970. But inflation does not affect all parts of a family's budget equally. It hits especially hard at food, health care, housing, and education. Moreover, as we saw in the previous chapter, there is something seriously wrong with the official index of purchasing power: It takes no account of the quality of goods and services. One can infer that women were going to work as much to replace or repair their cars, washing machines, and dishwashers as to acquire them. There was, after all, despite all the protestations of managerial innocence, an iron fist inside the glove of planned obsolescence. What good was it to own cars or dishwashers that kept breaking down? Critics of the American consumer's apparently insatiable appetite for cosmetic model changeovers fail to consider that while new seldom meant better, old usually meant broken. More and more, therefore, the wife's earnings had to be used for essentials rather than for frills and luxury items. Soon more and more baby-boom parents began to discover that if they wanted to enlarge their slice of the pie, or to just hold on to what they had, they could not do so on one salary. More and more the redemption of middle-class parenthood came down to one thing: a second income.

While I think I have now shown that there were strong economic pressures on women to break out of the homebody role, we must not forget the other side of the equation. Pressures to join the labor force have always existed, but married women had previously not yielded to them because there were simply no jobs they could or would take—no jobs that they themselves and their husbands and the other partisans of the marital and procreative imperative regarded as suitable for married women. Suitable jobs—jobs compatible with the traditional goals of procreation and marriage—would allow women to work part-time or to move in and out of the workforce in order to meet family needs. And if married women had to work, they should try not to compete with men and thereby cheapen the breadwinner's wages. They ought to work at occupations and industries in which women predominated.

Precisely these specifications characterize the jobs that went looking for women workers after World War II. As we have seen, the great bulk of the new jobs were of two types: low-level information-processing jobs such as file clerks, secretaries, typists, and receptionists; and low-level people-processing jobs such as nurses, primary school teachers, retail sales help, medical and dental assistants, guidance counsellors, and social workers. These were woman-dominated occupations, mainly part-time, in-and-out, temporary or dead-end, and almost always poorly paid as evidenced by the fact that the average employed woman in the United States makes only 58 percent of the average male's wages. Most of the new jobs were white- or "pink"-collar jobs and the great bulk of these, in turn, were secretarial, clerical, or sales jobs situated within or dependent on some branch of government or the bureaucracy of some large corporation or retail chain. In brief, the kinds of jobs that went looking for women were the jobs that were being created as an integral part of the process leading to the current bureaucratized and oligopolized impasse with its inconveniences, disservices and misinformation, and its inflationary inefficiencies.

In broad perspective, the call-up of women for duty in the service-and-information job market represents a curious replay of the call-up of women into manufacturing early in the industrial revolution. But there is one crucial difference: This time the recruitment of women for employment outside the home did not seem to threaten the livelihood of male workers since the kinds of jobs involved had long been dominated by women rather than men. They were jobs—at least at the beginning—that men didn't want and that married women took as a temporary expedient with their husband's approval in order to preserve the ideals of the marital and procreative imperative.

With the generation of immigrant "coolies" fading from the scene, the dormant white American housewife was the service-and-information employer's sleeping beauty. Her qualifications were superb. She was available in vast numbers. She had been trained for her entire life to be unaggressive and to take orders from men. Her husband earned more than she did so she would take a job that was neither permanent nor secure. She had little interest in joining a union and still less in struggling to form one. She would accept temporary jobs, part-time jobs, jobs that let her go home to cook or take care of the children, jobs that were boring, jobs that had no future. And she could read and write. All she needed was an office manager, agency head, financial vice president, or some other service-and-information-boss charming to kiss her into life.

The timing of the feminist outburst at the end of the 1960s marks the moment of collective realization that women, married or not, would have to continue to work as a consequence of inflation and of the growing dearth of males who held genuine breadwinner jobs, and that unless they rebelled they would continue to get the worst of all possible worlds: dull, boring, dead-end jobs at work, and cooking, cleaning, child care, and chauvinist males at home. At the end of the 1960s, women were being drawn through a pneumatic tube. At one end of the tube there was inflation squeezing them out of the home and into the job market; at the other end there was the expanding service-and-information job market, sucking them into a niche specifically designed for literate but inexpensive and docile workers who would accept 60 percent or less of what a man would want for the same job.

The pillars of the male-dominated breadwinner family now stood hollow and near collapse. Neither the interests of big business nor government lay as before in a united defense of the marital and procreative imperative. In an age of nuclear arms, high birthrates were no longer a military priority, while for government and business the immediate assured benefits of employing women overshadowed the long-run penalties of a falling birthrate. The only real opposition came from the organized churches. But here the struggle was waged with weapons of sentiment, and not those of material costs and benefits; and while the churches could make some couples feel guilty for not getting married and having children, they could scarcely offer to pay the bills for wives who felt guilty enough to stay home.

As for the male breadwinner, he least of all could resist the new role society was preparing for him. The Carnegie Corporation reports that "a family with an annual income of $10,000 must spend more than $50,000 to raise a child to the age of 18, not including savings put aside for higher education." Anthropologist Wanda Minge estimates that a moderate income family (with less than $20,000 after taxes) will have to spend $195,000 to rear a child from birth through four years of college, allowing for 10% annual inflation but no extras such as piano lessons or orthodontics. While married men on the average still contribute about three times as much as their work-

ing wives to family income, wives' salaries now make the
difference between just getting by or falling into poverty; or
between a barely middle-class versus a workingman's family
budget. As the *Wall Street Journal* put it: "The workingman
breadwinner who doesn't have a wife on a payroll just may
wind up not having enough bread." Or, one might add, breaking his back moonlighting on a second job.

To be sure, men wanted to keep women home and to have
their wives' paychecks too; they wanted wives to take care of
the kids *and* to go to work to help pay for them. And, to make
matters worse, they wanted the deference due the breadwinner without winning the bread. They wanted the kowtowing
and pandering of the old order to go on, as if a woman's well-
being still depended on finding, pleasing, and keeping a man
who could afford to get married.

Women were being asked to work in two places at once: to
work for half a man's pay on the job and for no pay at all off
the job, and to remain submissive and obedient to sexist husbands who no longer supported them. And so it was women
who had most to gain and least to lose by kicking at the hollow
pillars of the temple of marriage and childbirth.

The demise of the marital and procreative imperative has
brought about a rapid and irreversible restructuring of American domestic life and of the American way of love and sex.
Although authorities like historian Carl Degler and sociologist
Mary Jo Bane have tried to reassure the older generation that
the "family is here to stay," the family that remains is not the
family that the older generation wanted to preserve. Like it or
not, the lifetime male-dominated, two-parent, multichild,
breadwinner family has virtually ceased to exist. While it is
true that most children will continue to be born into some kind
of family situation, the kind of domestic unit involved and the
typical pattern of life experiences with respect to residence,
marriage, and child-rearing that Americans can look forward
to as they grow up are fundamentally new additions to American culture.

Much conservative thought about the preservation of traditional family patterns hinges on the notion that the precipitous drop in fertility is an aberration that will soon give way to another baby boom. Nothing of the sort is likely to occur. The baby boom was the aberration, the last hurrah of the marital and procreative imperative. As women struggle to achieve career parity with men and get ever more deeply involved in the job market, the historic downward trend in birthrates will continue for a long time to come. The rate mentioned earlier, the first-time marriage rate, has also been moving downward, falling from ninety per thousand single women in 1950 to about sixty-five in 1976. Most of this drop can be attributed to the aging baby-boom children who have been postponing marriage or not getting married at all. In 1960 only 28 percent of women between the ages of twenty and twenty-four were single; in 1974 the figure was 40 percent. And those who have gotten married have been getting divorced in astonishing numbers. Between 1965 and 1978 the country's divorce rate more than doubled with the highest frequency found again, significantly, among the younger, twenty-to-twenty-four age group. With one out of three marriages ending in divorce—an all-time high —it is farfetched to point to a high rate of remarriage among older couples (now also starting to decline) as evidence for the "preservation of the family." Very little is being preserved. Simultaneous with the rise in the divorce rate, the postponement of marriage, and the fall in the birthrate, there has been an 81 percent increase in the number of families headed by women—either separated, divorced, widowed, or never-married—since 1960. About 17 percent of all children now live in such families at any one time, and the odds that children born today will at one point be living in such families is well over 40 percent. As families grow smaller, as divorce rates rise and as marriage and birth rates fall, more and more Americans will find themselves living alone for a good portion of their lives. The growth in the number of single persons in the age group twenty-five to thirty-four is a forecast of things to come. In

1950 only one out of twenty men and women in this age group was living alone; in 1976, one out of three of them was living alone! Among elderly widowed women (sixty-five years and older), the frequency rose from one out of four to an astonishing two out of three. Already in 1980 only 6 percent of all American families fit the traditional normative pattern of full-time homebody wife and mother, breadwinner father and husband, and two or more dependent children. Far more Americans are living alone or in single-parent, remarried, or childless families than in the traditional nuclear family into which the baby-boom generation was born.

As I mentioned earlier, the change in the sexual composition of the labor force not only reshaped the American family but it has wrought profound changes in the nation's patterns of sexual behavior. It is to these further consequences of the rise of the service-and-information economy and the collapse of the marital and procreative imperative that we turn in the next chapter.

6

Why
the Gays
Came Out
of the
Closet

The patrons of Stonewall Inn, located at 53 Christopher Street in New York City's Greenwich Village, were dancing the frug, ogling the go-go boys, and "cruising" when the police burst through the doors. The raiders expected the usual. There might be some screaming and scratching as the "queens in drag" were hauled off to be booked for impersonating females, but the majority of the patrons would show their identification and then disappear as quickly and quietly as possible. But that is not what happened on Saturday night, June 29, 1969. Instead of slinking off, the ousted patrons gathered in front of the bar shouting and cursing. The crowd got bigger and when the "queens" came out screaming to be put in the van, the police were hit with a barrage of missiles ranging from pennies and stones to bricks and parking meters. Guns drawn, the raiders retreated into the bar and called for reinforcements. Bricks flew, glass shattered, and fires burned out of control for three nights.

Historians of gay liberation celebrate the Stonewall Riots as the "raid heard round the world." June 28, 1969, was "the day the worm turned," or to approximate the words of homosexual poet Allen Ginsberg, "the day the fags lost their scared look." The Gay Liberation Front was founded in New York a few days later and soon similar groups in other cities were preaching "gay pride," "zapping" the police, and lobbying for pro-homosexual candidates and legislation, aided by a gay liberationist press that had sprung up almost overnight—*Come Out* in New York, *Fag Rag* in Boston, *Gay Sunshine* in San Francisco—all with the same message: It was time for homosexuals to stop hating themselves; homosexuality was not a disease, a "perversion," or an inferior form of sexuality. On the contrary, homosexuals enjoyed life more and were better human beings than the average "straight." One should be proud to be a homosexual. Attempts to hide one's true sexual preferences must cease. Gay men and women who pretended that they were straight hindered the struggle for sexual self-determination, perpetuated discriminatory hiring and firing practices, and nourished the seedy underworld of homosexual bars, sexual blackmail, and police shakedowns. Carl Wittman's *Gay Manifesto* captured the spirit of the post-Stonewall age. The time had come to stop running away:

> We have fled from blackmailing cops, from families who disowned or "tolerate" us; we have been drummed out of the armed services, thrown out of schools, fired from jobs, beaten by punks and policemen. . . . We have pretended everything is OK, because we haven't been able to see how to change it—we've been afraid.

Comparing "closet queens" to Uncle Toms among blacks, Wittman's manifesto called upon all homosexuals to step out of the closet:

> To pretend to be straight sexually, or to pretend to be straight socially, is probably the most harmful pattern of behavior in the

99

ghetto. The married guy who makes it on the side secretly; the guy who will go to bed once but won't develop any gay relationships; the pretender at school who changes the gender of the friend he's talking about. . . . If we are liberated we are open about our sexuality. Closet queenery must end. Come out.

And they did come out. More accurately, they poured out. Bewildered straight America suddenly found itself living alongside a homosexual second society, a segregated parallel social world that had sprung up in every large city and many smaller ones, that involved several million men and women, hundreds of organizations, and billions of dollars' worth of businesses. By 1980 the United States and Canada had acquired the largest, best-organized, and most powerful homosexual minority in the history of the world.

The most significant feature of the gay community is what researcher John Lee calls its "institutional completeness"— the ability of contemporary liberated gay men or women to go through life using businesses and services dominated by or dedicated to homosexual needs. Here is Lee's description of how a homosexual citizen can make use of gay institutions in any large American city:

A gay citizen . . . can buy a home through a gay real estate agent familiar with the types of housing and neighborhoods most suitable to gay clients. He can close the deal through a gay lawyer, and insure with a gay insurance agent. If he is new to the community and cannot ask acquaintances for the names of these agents, he can consult the Gay Yellow Pages, a listing of businesses and services which is available in many larger cities. Or he can approach a typical source of connection with the gay community, such as a gay bookstore, or he can consult a local gay newspaper or periodical. From any of these sources of information he will also learn where he can buy lumber and renovating supplies from a company catering to a gay clientele. He will find gay suppliers of furniture, houseplants, and interior decorating. He will find gay sources of skilled labour or gay cleaning services.

Having moved in, our gay citizen can clothe himself at gay-oriented clothing stores, have his hair cut by a gay stylist, his spectacles made by a gay optician. He can buy food at a gay bakery, records at a gay phonograph shop, and arrange his travel plans through gay travel agents. He can buy newspapers and books at a gay bookstore, worship in a gay church or synagogue, and eat at gay restaurants. Naturally he can drink at gay bars and dance at gay discotheques. He can obtain medical care from a gay physician or if he prefers, a gay chiropractor. If he wishes to remain entirely within the gay culture, he can seek work at many of these agencies and businesses, but he will have to bank his earnings at a nongay bank,* though he may be able to deal with a gay credit union. He can contribute money to tax-deductible gay foundations, participate in gay political groups, and enjoy gay-produced programs on cable television. To keep him up to date on everything happening in his gay community he can telephone the Gay Line, which is updated weekly.

Lee's sketch does not pretend to be comprehensive. The New York-New Jersey edition of *Gayellow Pages* contains ninety-six pages of listings and advertisements which invite homosexuals to patronize gay antique stores and art galleries, lesbian radio shows, an Old Blue Women's Rugby Club, lesbian theaters, a lesbian weight-reduction clinic, gay tax accountants, gay ad agencies, gay telephone answering services, gay astrologers, gay car rentals, a gay carpet store, gay computer services, gay dentists, gay exterminators, gay plumbers, gay carpenters, gay electricians, gay insurance companies, gay private eyes, gay investment bankers, a gay motorcycle club, and a gay piano tuner. There are even special provisions for homosexual parents including "Dykes 'n' Tykes," and the "Gay Daddies of Westchester."

Like women's liberationists, gays attribute their sudden militancy to the contagious spread of rebellion from the civil rights movement, the anti-Vietnam war protests, and the "counter-culture." "The 'New Left' of the 1960s aggregated the rising discontent of black people, women, and a generation of young men sent by the United States government to Viet-

* A gay-owned bank opened in San Francisco in 1980.

nam," explains Barry D. Adam. "The new militance provided
new precedents for a reevaluation of the oppression of gay
people." In the preamble to his *Gay Manifesto,* Carl Wittman
is less certain: "How it began we don't know; maybe we were
inspired by black people and their freedom movement; we
learned how to stop pretending from the hip revolution. Amer-
ika in all its ugliness has surfaced with the war and our national
leaders." But Dennis Altman in his book *Homosexual Oppression and Liberation* emphatically declares: "Without the
example provided by the blacks, the young radicals, the
women's movement, gay liberation could not have been
born."

Altman claims that gays needed the example of other rebellious movements because homosexuals had accepted the idea
that they were sick and perverted and lived in a furtive underworld oblivious of being oppressed. But self-blame and a lack
of awareness are "marks of oppression"—a phrase originally
applied to segregated blacks—that minorities always find hard
to struggle against: Witness the endless consciousness-raising
rap sessions among the feminists. If Altman's point is that
homosexuals were more oppressed than blacks or women, it
does not follow that they should have rebelled last. On the
contrary, one might just as well expect them to rebel first,
given all the beatings, jailings, and humiliation they had to
endure.

I think gay liberation is more than a sequence of historic
accidents connecting one form of frustrated or indignant
human consciousness with another. Once again, there is a
deeper institutional causal level that must be taken into account, one that relates the rise of the American homosexual
community to the rise of the service-and-information economy, the recruitment of married women into the labor force,
and the collapse of the marital and procreative imperative and
of the male breadwinner family.

The linkage between women going to work and gays coming
out of the closet will become clearer if we ask ourselves why

gays were in the closet in the first place. Some people suppose that it is only "natural" for a society to try to suppress homosexual forms of sex. No doubt most human beings experience a strong erotic attraction to the opposite sex that is rooted in human nature (although the social environment obviously shapes this attraction, and determines what kind of heterosexual activity, if any, it will lead to). But why should the natural predominance of heterosexual impulses lead to tabooing homosexual impulses and making them a crime? One possibility is that along with the natural preference for the opposite sex, most people also have a natural aversion for the same sex. But that seems unlikely. There is a lot of evidence that men and women acquire their aversion to homosexual sex in the course of growing up and being molded by social customs and conditions. This is not to say that all heterosexuals are potential or repressed homosexuals—the categories are misleading—but that people easily learn to accept homosexual forms of sexuality if there are social precedents or personal advantages to be derived from it. Few human beings can be described either as "obligative" heterosexuals or "obligative" homosexuals, that is, as individuals for whom any deviation from the pattern of exclusive heterosexuality or exclusive homosexuality is suppressed by powerful innate drives. As researchers C. S. Ford and F. A. Beach concluded after studying the incidence of homosexuality around the world, "Human homosexuality is not basically a product of hormonal imbalance or 'perverted' heredity. It is the product of the fundamental mammalian heritage of general sexual responsiveness as modified under the impact of experience."

A description of the sex practices of some societies that expect or demand homosexual relationships may be helpful here. One of the better-known examples is the ancient Greeks. We know that almost all of the familiar figures in Greek philosophy and politics engaged in a form of homosexuality in which older males had sexual intercourse with younger men or boys. The preferred form of intercourse was for the senior to place his penis between the junior's thighs. (Anal intercourse was commonly practiced only between men and women or between men who were of unequal social rank.) For teachers such as Socrates and his students Plato and Xenophon, sex was an integral part of the educational process intended to facilitate the transfer of knowledge from an active loving teacher to a passive junior student.

Greek homosexuality with its characteristic senior-junior relationship seems to have been modeled after a still more ancient and pervasive practice indulged in by Greek warriors. We know that many Greek soldiers took boys along with them on the march who served as sleeping companions and sex partners, while learning the martial arts. The Theban military corps known as the Sacred Band gained its strength from the homosexual unity of male warrior couples. And both Plato and Xenophon indicate that senior and junior homosexual partners fighting side by side made the best fighting force. As the philosopher Jeremy Bentham pointed out to the dismay of Victorian scholars who refused to believe that their Greek heroes were eager homosexuals: "Everybody practiced it; nobody was ashamed of it. They might be ashamed of what they looked upon as an excess in it, or they might be ashamed of it as a weakness, as a propensity that had a tendency to distract men from more worthy and important occupations . . . but in itself one may be sure that they were not ashamed of it."

Despite their enthusiasm for male lovers, the men of ancient Greece were not obligative homosexuals. Most of them were also staunch supporters of marriage and the family. All male citizens were expected to get married, sleep with their wives, and have children. That her husband enjoyed having sex with young boys was of little concern to the Greek wife as long as he also slept with her, treated her kindly, and provided for the children. Contrary to popular stereotypes about male homosexuals in the United States, Greek men who had homosexual relationships were not considered effeminate; everyone thought it was the manly thing to do.

Similar forms of what might be called "supplementary homosexuality" occur in many parts of the world, each with its own special social and sexual attributes adapted to local contexts. Among the Azande, a people of the Southern Sudan, supplementary homosexuality mirrors the Greek pattern in certain ways, but departs from it in other interesting respects. The Azande were divided into separate warring principalities, each of which maintained a corps of young bachelors as a standing military force. These young warriors traditionally "married" boys and satisfied their sexual needs with them during their early years of military service before they were able to pay the "brideprice" needed to marry a woman. Boy marriage mirrored aspects of regular Azande woman marriage. The groom gave a token brideprice of five or more spears to the boy's parents. The boy addressed the senior man as "my husband," ate out of sight of the warriors just as women ate out of sight of their husbands, gathered leaves for the senior man's daily toilet and for his bed at night, and brought him water, firewood, and food. In addition, while on the march the boy-wife carried the warrior's shield. At night the two slept together. As among the Greeks, the sex act was intended to satisfy the senior partner and, like the Greeks, the Azande senior placed his penis between the boy's thighs. "The boys got what pleasure they could by friction of their organs on the husband's belly or groin." Like early Greek senior-junior intercourse, Azande homosexuality was a form of military apprenticeship. As the bachelor warriors grew older, they gave up their boy-wives, paid brideprice for a woman—several if they could afford it, for the Azande were polygynous—and fathered many children. Meanwhile, the former boy-wives entered the ranks of the bachelor corps and married a new set of boy-brides. The British anthropologist E. E. Evans-Pritchard, who took down this information from Azande informants, emphasizes the supplementary or secondary nature of Azande homosexuality. "As in ancient Greece, so far as one can judge, when the boy-wives grew up and when they and their husbands married females they had a normal (for the Azande) married life like everyone else." Azande informants bluntly characterized the taking of boy-wives as an adaptation to the practical problems confronted by the young Azande male. Since older men married several women at a time, there was a shortage of female wives for the junior men (who also depended on the seniors to pay brideprice).

Among the most thoroughly homosexual societies known are the Etoro of New Guinea. As reported by anthropologist Raymond Kelly, the Etoro believe that semen is a precious life-giving fluid which each man possesses in limited supply. Without semen, a man withers and dies. This in itself is not an unusual doctrine; many modern-day Hindus in India believe that a man is born with a fixed supply of semen. In order to mature and live to a ripe old age, one must carefully conserve this supply throughout life and not waste it by masturbating or by having intercourse too frequently after getting married. In the last century similar beliefs were common in Europe and the United States where medical authorities warned sexually hyperactive males against the ill effects of "spending" their semen. What is radically different about the Etoro is their notion of how a man acquires his semen supply. They believe that it can be acquired only as a gift that one male bestows on another. To ensure that semen is properly distributed and used for worthy social purposes, older Etoro men are expected to transfer their semen to young boys. This is done by penis-to-mouth intercourse (fellatio) between seniors and juniors respectively, who sleep together in a village men's quarters—a separate large house—from which all females are barred. This part of the Etoro system again is similar to the relationship of Azande men to their boy-wives or of Greek philosophers to their pupils. The senior Etoro male not only nourishes his boy consort—the semen makes the boy grow and mature—but he teaches him the secrets of Etoro religion and the art of manly combat. Etoro seniors are deeply concerned that some youths may cheat on the system and that they will attempt to augment

106

their semen intake by "stealing" semen from their age mates through illicit affairs. A young man who matures very quickly and shows a lack of deference to his seniors will come under suspicion as one who is getting more than his proper share of seminal nourishment. If a youth persists in such antisocial practices, he may be accused of witchcraft and be severely punished or killed.

The worst threat to the Etoro male's peace of mind is the temptation to have intercourse with women. All Etoro men get married, but they are forbidden to have intercourse with their wives for from 205 to 260 days each year and then only in the forest far away from their houses, villages, and crops. Wives must be careful not to make sexual overtures to their husbands, lest they too be accused of conspiring to steal the precious seminal substance.

Unfortunately, anthropologists have not acquired as much information about female as about male homosexuals. In some polygynous societies such as the Azande, wives whose husbands are inattentive have clandestine lesbian relationships. But since males usually dominate the means of physical and psychological repression, relatively few instances of lesbianism have come to light. (Also, most anthropologists have been males and have not been willing or able to talk with women informants.)

Anthropological studies do show quite conclusively nonetheless that relatively few societies place a complete ban on all types of homosexual activities. Therefore, the appropriate question to be asked about societies that instill an aversion to all forms of homosexuality and force their gays into the closet is not why homosexual behavior sometimes occurs (a favorite but misguided theme of psychiatrists, social scientists, and homosexuals themselves), but why it doesn't occur more often. Not why some people find it appealing, but why so many people find it appalling.

Anthropologist Dennis Werner of the Graduate School of the City University of New York has made an important discovery about societies that taboo homosexuality versus those that practice it as a supplementary form of sex. Werner divided a sample of thirty-nine societies into two groups, pro-natalists and anti-natalists. The pro-natalists were societies that, like the U.S.A., banned abortion and infanticide; the anti-natalists were societies that permitted abortion or infanticide for nonadulterous married women. Werner found that male homosexuality was frowned upon, ridiculed, scorned, or punished for all segments of the population in 75 percent of the pro-natalist societies and that it was permitted or encouraged for at least some people in 60 percent of the anti-natalist societies. The inescapable conclusion is this: The aversion to homosexuality is greatest where the marital and procreative imperative is strongest.

Western society in the Judeo-Christian tradition fits this formula to perfection. Throughout most of European and American history we have been consummate procreationists. The biblical injunction to multiply and fill the earth and subdue it has been spelled out in countless laws, repressive acts, and moral precepts directed not only against abortion, contraception, and infanticide, but against any form of nonprocreative sex—not only against homosexuality but against masturbation, pederasty, fellatio, or cunnilingus, regardless of whether performed by a man and woman or regardless of whether performed in or out of wedlock, as we saw in the preceding chapter.

The peculiar ferocity bordering on hysteria that has characterized traditional American attempts to suppress homosexual intercourse (as well as other anti-natalist activities) deserves special comment. Following the analysis presented in the previous chapter, it seems likely that the temptation for people to engage in homosexual (as well as other nonprocreative) forms of sex will increase in direct proportion to the adverse balance of costs and benefits associated with the rearing of children; or in other words, when there is pressure on people to lower the birthrate. Note that this is not the same as saying that homosexuality or other forms of nonprocreative sex will occur *only* when there is such pressure. Not at all. Some form or degree of homosexuality can be expected in almost any human society under a multitude of conditions (illustrated by the Greek and Azande cases, neither of which is strongly anti-natalist). Rather, the point is that to the extent that homosexuality and other nonprocreative forms of sex are already present, their incidence and variety will tend to increase if people feel increasing pressure to reduce the number of their children.

If a society is strongly pro-natalist to begin with and has a long-standing tradition of opposing nonprocreative sex, the movement to lower the birthrate may not immediately result in easing or lifting pro-natalist taboos. In the short run, the contrary may happen, especially if there are powerful segments of the society that continue to benefit from and insist upon high general rates of population growth. In these conditions, instead of leading to greater sexual freedom, the threat to the birthrate may at first simply provoke a reaction leading to ferocious and bizarre forms of sexual repression.

It is this reaction I think which accounts for the peculiar sexual mores of what we call the Victorian era in Britain and the United States. During this era (which actually lasted well into the twentieth century) prudery rose as the birthrate fell. The attempt to enforce the procreative and marital imperative became so extreme that the very words for nonprocreative sexual acts were taboo. Even doctors hesitated to utter them or to write them down in medical textbooks. The veil of secrecy about such matters became so thick that lawmakers and judges as well as ordinary citizens lost their ability even to have coherent discussions about them. Onanism, for example, which in the Bible simply refers to Onan's ejaculation on the ground after withdrawing from intercourse with his brother's wife, got confused with masturbation. And masturbation lost its specific meaning when doctors and preachers used it to designate almost any form of male or female homosexuality. Every state enacted laws against sodomy, but the prosecution sometimes failed to get convictions because the legislators had shied away from defining what they meant by the term. This loss was more than compensated by the aura of fear and loathing that rises when horrors are left to the imagination. The Victorians' reluctance to discuss sexual matters, their ignorance concerning the anatomy and functions of the sex organs, and their propensity to blush or faint simply upon hearing the vernacular words for sexual intercourse are all understandable from the same perspective: an increased need to repress nonprocreative sex in order to counter the increasing temptation to violate the marital and procreative imperative.

This view accounts for some of the oft-noted paradoxes of the Victorian era. Despite all of the efforts to repress nonprocreative and nonmarital sex, we know that in the mid-to-late nineteenth century prostitution flourished as never before in every big American city and that there was a brisk secret trade in pornographic books. From the hysterical warning against onanism—"the Onanist distills a poison onto his frame that will inevitably, if not relieved by timely aid, lead to his death," ranted George C. Calhoun—and from the draconian measures advocated to cure it—castration; clitoridectomy; circumcision; blistering of the thighs, vulva, or prepuce—one can reasonably infer that people must have been secretly masturbating and sodomizing more frequently. What appears to us as inexcusable Victorian sham and hypocrisy therefore may best be seen as a manifestation of an escalating conflict between anti-natalist and pro-natalist forces. And since much of this conflict was played out in the minds of the people who stood to lose from obeying the marital and procreative imperative—men and women who could not afford to have children or even to get married—small wonder that women tended to faint at the sight of a penis and that some men and women actually did go crazy from masturbating and felt sick and depraved if they preferred homosexuality to abstinence, solitary masturbation, or prostitution.

The hysterical intensity with which homosexuality was repressed during the Victorian period has much to do with the

110

specific militant content of the gay movement. The ban on homosexual sex was so complete, and the odium attached to it so strong, that even a single homosexual performance was sufficient to brand a person for life as a pervert or degenerate. Instead of making way for homosexuality as a supplementary or secondary form of sexual pleasure, the American Victorians insisted that only the most depraved persons could so much as contemplate homosexual intercourse. From this there developed the peculiar notion that homosexuality is not a type of activity, but a state of being; that people are either in a heterosexual state of being or a homosexual state of being; and that if they are in a homosexual state of being, they are a depraved type of person whom other people ought to shun.

And so when the time came for homosexuals to rebel against prudery and oppression—to come out of the closet—they did so, not as individuals defending homosexuality as a supplement to heterosexuality, but as a group dedicated to forming an exclusively homosexual community with a total homosexual way of life.

The question remains as to why the Stonewall Rebellion took place in 1969. Just as the birthrate kept coming down, despite all the marital and procreative laws aimed at achieving the opposite, repression and prudery could not prevent large numbers of people from clandestinely experimenting with homosexual sex as an alternative to bachelorhood, spinsterhood, and procreative marriages. Dennis Werner's basic theory implies that any strengthening of the anti-natalist position tends to increase the practice of homosexuality. Women's liberation, as we have seen, was itself made possible by a major shift in the balance of power between anti- and pro-natalist forces—a shift rooted in the rapidly changing character of the U.S. labor force. During 1960–1970 the same shift provided powerful incentives for rapid growth of the nonobligative homosexual population in the United States and for the migration of homosexuals from all over the country into emergent gay ghettos.

Sociologist Martin Levine has pointed out that gays formed

ghettos much as other pariah castes and minorities have formed them, for conviviality and self-defense. Gay ghettos contain a large number of institutions catering to homosexuals —businesses, bars, restaurants, clubs, meeting spaces, and cruising areas—a substantial gay population, and a locally dominant gay way of life (for example, same-sex couples embracing on the street without attracting attention). In five cities studied, Levine found that the neighborhoods that met the criteria for being fully developed gay ghettos were the West Village in New York, Castro Village in San Francisco, and "Boys Town" (West Hollywood), Los Angeles. But he also found twelve additional neighborhoods that seem on the verge of becoming homosexual ghettos. While gay liberation speeded the formation of gay ghettos, the nucleus of each of the major ones had probably already formed before the Stonewall Riots. Certainly the sheer density of homosexuals in the West Village in 1969 made it more difficult for the police to control the mobs that took to the streets each night.

The timing of the Stonewall Riots therefore was governed by a convergence of conditions favorable to adopting an exclusionist homosexual life-style. On the one side there were all the anti-natalist sentiments unleashed by married women's entrance into the wage labor force and all the penalties associated with the male-centered breadwinner family in an increasingly inefficient and inflationary economy plagued by high unemployment. On the other side there was the slow buildup of homosexual pre-ghetto neighborhoods by closet gays looking for alternatives to marriage, abstinence, solitary masturbation, bachelorhood, and spinsterhood. The other liberationist movements may have provided the spark, but without the anti-natalist structural tinder the flames would have fizzled as they had always done in the past.

In other words, gay liberation accompanied women's liberation because each movement represents a different facet of the collapse of the marital and procreative imperative and the male-dominated breadwinner family. Homosexuality in its exclusionist form is the radical left wing of the anti-natalist movement. The prominent role of lesbian activists in women's liberation makes this clear. Lesbians in NOW and other organizations have repeatedly attacked heterosexual feminists for "collaborating with the enemy." According to the lesbian militants, men cannot help but be opposed to women's liberation and therefore women ought to sever all intimate and supportive relationships with them, especially those involving sex, marriage, and reproduction. The antiparenthood theme in radical lesbian feminism aims to "demystify" women's reproductive functions. Pregnancy, "a temporary deformation of the body for the sake of the species," is an affliction of "fat ladies" caused by a "tenant," "parasite," or "uninvited guest." "Childbirth is painful and hideous. Motherhood is portrayed as a condition of terminal psychological and social decay, total self-abnegation and physical deterioration." Obviously only a small minority of feminists hold such extreme views, but to judge from the plunging birthrates, the message has not been entirely lost.

Despite their consciousness of themselves as people fighting for a sexual rather than a reproductive preference, nonobligative gays are also very much involved in the struggle to throw off the yoke of parenthood. Exclusive homosexuals enjoy the ultimate in contraceptive protection, no matter how relentless their search of orgasms, no matter how often they change partners. (There are some gay mothers and fathers but most of them became parents during an earlier heterosexual period in their lives. Very few gay men or women are now or ever want to be parents. In San Francisco, for example, in a population of several hundred thousand gays, Lesbian Mothers and Friends has only 130 members while Gay Fathers has less than 60 members.)

With the end of the baby boom, the floodgates of nonmarital and nonprocreative sex swung open to accommodate the childless working man and childless working woman. Out rushed all of the secret and long-abominated sex practices and sentiments of which homosexuality is but one instance. From the pages of best-seller marriage manuals on the joys of sex to

113

the centerfolds of *Penthouse, Playboy,* and *Playgirl,* the hard-core message is that sex does not, need not, should not lead to reproduction. Suddenly there was a vast industry of X-rated movies designed for dates at the drive-ins. Fortunes were made from films and videotape cassettes depicting every conceivable form of sexual excitement brought home for private viewing. Survey reports of women's sex habits became best sellers. Women learned that there are six basic ways to masturbate and that " 'It's nice to have fun all by yourself.' " Comic books for teenagers extolled the virtues of "Tits n' Clits." Not to mention the huge growth industry in massage parlors, swinger clubs, escort services, live sex shows, adult bookstores, and porno joints where men who can't afford anything better can sit in little booths and masturbate.

The other side of the message that sex is for pleasure and not for reproduction is that parents have no fun. Have the joys of parenthood ever been viewed with more jaundiced eyes than by America's "me only" generation? According to a study carried out by the consumer research firm of Yankelovich, Skelly and White, Americans now rate new cars over children on their list of items deemed necessary for the good life. "It is not a question of whether children are sweet and marvelous to have and rear," wrote one feminist, "the question is, even if that's so, whether or not one wants to pay the price for it. It doesn't make sense anymore to pretend that women need babies, when what they really need is themselves." According to the National Alliance for Optional Parenthood, in 1967 only one percent of wives between the ages of eighteen and twenty-four did not expect to have a child. By 1977 this figure had changed to 5 percent. A phenomenal 11 percent of all women between eighteen and thirty-four now plan to remain childless.

Why then did women's liberation, gay liberation, and sexual liberation burst upon the American scene at the same time? I think the answer is that they were each a different facet of a single process. Each was a response to the rapid buildup of a negative balance of cost and benefit in the breadwinner family. What each bears witness to in a slightly different form is the

114

reshaping of America's mode of reproducing itself to accord with the limitations and opportunities of an increasingly inefficient economy in which both men and women must work and both must work away from home.

Belatedly, feminists have begun to grasp the systemic implications for reproduction and parenthood of their struggle to achieve parity with men in the workforce. Betty Friedan who once described suburban housewifery as life in a "comfortable concentration camp" insists that feminists never intended to create a situation that was unfavorable to having children. Their intention was rather to give women the right to be able to work and love in equality with men and to choose, if they so desire, to have children. But now that choice is "not as simple as it once seemed" because of the "unanticipated conflicts between the demands of the workplace and professional success on the one hand, and the demands of the family on the other." Still laboring under the misapprehension that it was consciousness-raising by women's liberationists that stirred the denizens of suburban concentration camps to go out and find jobs for themselves, Friedan now admits that the freedom supposedly won for women is illusory.

> I don't envy young women who are facing or denying that agonizing choice we won for them. Because it isn't really a free choice when their paycheck is needed to cover the family bills each month, when women must look to their jobs and professions for the security and status their mothers once sought in marriage alone, and when these professions are not structured for people who give birth to children and take responsibility for their upbringing.

I hope I have succeeded in clarifying the causal connections that link new forms of sex and family life to the role of women in the labor force and ultimately to America's new people—and information-processing economy. If so, it is time to broaden our perspective to include two other dimensions of cultural crisis—crime and the welfare mess—which are also closely linked to the same causal web.

7

Why There's Terror on the Streets

Surveys show that more than a fifth of the inhabitants of America's largest cities feel "very unsafe" when they go out at night, even in their own neighborhoods. Women and old people have the greatest fear. Over half of all U.S. women say they are afraid to go out alone after dark. Senior citizens are afraid to leave their apartments during the day. People even feel insecure indoors: one-third of all U.S. households contain firearms purchased for protection against intruders.

Victims of violent crimes such as muggings or rapes have nightmares, uncontrollable phobias, hysterical fits of crying, long after the event. Even a simple case of breaking and entering in which the thief does not confront the victim can leave people in a state of shock. One suddenly feels exposed and vulnerable. That a stranger has penetrated unbidden into the sanctuary of one's home and taken away personal possessions creates a sense of helplessness and bereavement out of proportion to the value of the property or the amount of money that has been stolen.

Statistics cannot measure the impact of violent crime on our lives. No one knows how many people have moved to the suburbs primarily to escape from crime-ridden neighborhoods. And it is impossible to take account of all the things we do each day to guard against muggers, rapists, and other violent criminals. Our "fine-tuning" against the threat of attack adds up to a heavy psychological and physical burden. For example, think of all the extra locks and bolts we have to contend with each day, the peepholes we have to look through, all the mirrors and TV monitors in the hallways and elevators that we have to watch. Think how often we worry about our wallets in crowded places and of how tightly we clutch our handbags while shopping. If we have to drive through certain neighborhoods, we keep the doors locked and windows rolled up. We are always signing in and signing out, showing photos or badges, or hunting for the right key. We make long detours to get from one place to another because doors are locked, gates are shut, passageways closed. We try to park in busy, brightly lit areas. We hurry out at the end of movies and shows. And when we have to walk on a dark street we monitor ahead and behind and cross from one side to the other, watching for shadows in doorways. In his book *Mugging: You Can Protect Yourself,* police officer Liddon Griffith recommends that late moviegoers have their car key on the ready and that they walk past the car to make sure that no one is hiding in the back seat. Griffith advises men and women to keep small change available in their pockets and never to open their purses or wallets in public. It is dangerous to attract attention by seeming to be anxious about wallets or handbags. Women should not clutch their bags too tightly because if they try to hold on the purse snatchers will hit them. So Griffith advises city women to drill a minute a day at not freezing their grip on their purse when taken by surprise. Griffith also does not think it's unreasonable for men and women to study self-defense. In some situa-

117

tions, one's life may depend on being able to stun the attacker. Griffith urges city dwellers to learn how to reach behind an attacker's legs and pinch him on the inside of the thigh or grab his testicles and squeeze them.

Are all these fears justified? In 1973 the Law Enforcement Assistance Administration with the cooperation of the Bureau of the Census initiated an annual series of *crime victimization* studies. The Bureau interviews about sixty thousand people twice a year to find out if they have been the victims of criminal activity during a given period. The crime victimization studies indicate that annually there are over 4 million victims of assaults, a million victims of personal robberies (not including victims robbed in commercial establishments), 145,000 victims of rapes or attempted rapes, and 150,000 victims of purse snatchings. The crime victimization surveys do not provide information on homicides (for obvious reasons), but according to the FBI's annual Uniform Crime Report, there are about 20,000 homicides per year. (Criminologists regard this as one of the most accurate crime statistics, since murders rarely fail to attract the attention of law enforcement officers.)

One can see how much violent crime there is in the U.S.A. by comparing U.S. crime rates with those in other advanced industrial societies. Using only the FBI's figures and considering only crimes reported to the police, we find there are proportionately five times more homicides, ten times more rapes, and seventeen times more robberies in the United States than in Japan; and there are proportionately seven times more homicides, twelve times more rapes, and eight times more robberies in the United States than in Great Britain. These differences are just as great if we compare on a city by city basis. London and Tokyo, for example, have far less violent crime than less populous American cities such as Chicago, Philadelphia, or St. Louis.

Can these differences be explained by different methods of reporting crimes? Both the Japanese and the British have nationally centralized criminal justice systems which receive direct notification of all reported crimes, while the U.S.A. has 15,000 separate law enforcement bodies which process their own statistics and then forward them to the FBI. If anything, then, the British and Japanese figures are more accurate than the FBI's.

Another issue that must be clarified is whether the amount of criminal violence in the U.S.A. has been increasing. Are we really in the midst of a "crime wave"? The FBI's Uniform Crime Report indicates that the robbery rate went up by over 500 percent from 1945 to 1975, while in the two decades since 1960 the rate of all "violent crimes"—murder, rape, robbery, and aggravated assault—rose about half as fast. The latest FBI figures show that after a brief decline in 1975, the rate has resumed its merry ascent with a 13 percent gain between 1978 and 1979. Yet some insiders insist that there really is no crime wave going on.

The best evidence for this view is that the new crime victimization studies show no substantial increase in victimizations between 1973 and 1979. Since it is clear that the police and the FBI have known or reported less than half of the crimes that criminals actually commit, the annual rise in the FBI's reported crime rate could conceivably represent nothing more than an increase in the willingness or ability of victims to report crimes, or an increase in the willingness or ability of the police to find out about and record criminal acts. But the crime victimization studies have certain drawbacks and limitations. First of all, the fact that they did not get started until 1973 means that they cannot be used as a check on the FBI's statistics for a crucial portion of the post-war period. Second, the FBI's reported rise in murder rate must be taken as hard data for reasons already mentioned. Third, part of the discrepancy between the data from the victimization studies and the data from the FBI may have something to do with the fact that children under twelve years of age are not included in the victimization sample, yet a disproportionate share of recent increases in criminal violence may involve attacks by teen-agers against subteens. While a portion of the FBI's reported increase in criminal violence, therefore, may result from dip-ping into the reservoir of previously undetected or unreported crimes, there is no justification for attributing *all* of the re-ported increase to aberrant statistics. After all, one could cut the FBI's reported rate of increase in half, and still have legit-imate grounds for talking about a wave of violent crime in the United States since 1945.

The argument so far has been mainly concerned with two deceptively simple points: America, compared with other in-dustrial countries, has an unusually high level of certain kinds of violent crimes, and the level of such crimes has been in-creasing rapidly since 1945. What is the explanation for this?

The fact that violent crimes are more common in the U.S.A. than in countries like Japan and Great Britain casts doubt on several popular theories about crime in the United States. The first theory is that criminal violence is simply an inevitable manifestation of the capitalist mode of production. This theory fails to account for the peculiarly low rate of crime in Japan and Great Britain (not to mention Holland and Switzerland which have some of the lowest rates of violent crime in the world) which are also capitalist countries. The second theory is that violent crime in the United States is simply the result of urbanization. Clearly this theory is also inadequate because both Great Britain and Japan are highly urbanized. In 1979 there were 279 times as many robberies, 14 times as many rapes, and 12 times as many murders in New York City than in Tokyo which is the world's largest city.

The comparison between violent crime rates in the United States and in other countries also undermines the popular no-tion that we have a high crime rate because we are "too soft on criminals." This idea is very attractive because it points to a relatively simple solution to the crime problem: Build more jails and fill them up. Unfortunately there is no way to connect the United States's relatively high crime rates with a corre-sponding relative lack of punishment for crimes. The United

States has a bigger percentage of its population in jail (for nonpolitical offenses) than any country in the world. In 1978 the rate of imprisonment stood at over two hundred prisoners for each one hundred thousand people, which is two and a half times higher than the rate of imprisonment in Great Britain and five times higher than the rate of imprisonment in Japan. If any conclusion were to be drawn from these figures, it would have to be that the high rate of U.S. crime is caused by the peculiarly high rate of imprisonment characteristic of our criminal justice system. And this is not as far-fetched as it seems at first sight. The theory that prisons cause crime has its supporters. Prisons, some say, are "schools for crime" where the inmates are stigmatized for life and learn to become hardened criminals.

But it is not only what criminals find inside prisons that inclines them to commit crimes; it is also what they find when they get out. Without changing both parts of the equation, abolishing jails would not abolish criminal behavior. On the contrary, if the gates of every prison were suddenly to swing open, there would be a massive upward leap in criminal violence. Who can doubt that?

If one accepts the reported escalating crime rates as genuine indicators of increasing crime, several additional popular theories about the causes of violent crime in the United States also become less believable. These are the "culture" or "national character" theories which hold that traditions of lawlessness and violence got started during America's frontier days and have become part of a permanent national heritage. "Tradition" might explain why America's rate of criminal violence is higher than England's or Japan's, but it can scarcely explain why it is higher today than in 1945. If the FBI's figures mean anything, back in 1945 the rate of violent crime in the United States was not very different from what it is in Japan and England today. Tradition cannot explain something that has changed so fast; something that has changed so fast is obviously not a tradition.

But there is another kind of tradition argument that has to

121

be taken more seriously. The American Constitution guarantees citizens the right to bear arms, and this has made it possible for U.S. criminals to obtain firearms more readily than their counterparts in countries like Japan and England. Since it is far easier to kill someone with a gun than with other weapons, the high rate of homicide in the United States undoubtedly reflects, to some extent, the estimated 50 million handguns and rifles legally and illegally owned by the American people. One can see how assaults motivated by jealous quarrels and personal conflicts are more likely to have lethal results in the United States than in countries that ban the use of firearms. And as there has been a steady increase in the availability of firearms since 1945, this may account for much of the increase in the homicide rate. But the contribution made by the increased possession of firearms to the rising rate of robbery and rape is not so clear. The majority of rapes and robberies do not involve any weapons; and when the offenders in these crimes use weapons they are more likely to use knives or clubs than guns. Incidentally, the frequency of injury during a rape or robbery is lower when offenders use guns rather than knives, probably because the victims are less likely to fight back.

Why then is the rate of violent crime so much higher in the United States than in other industrial capitalist countries? And why has that rate increased so much since World War II? I think that the answer to both questions lies in the fact that America has developed a unique permanent racial underclass consisting of millions of impoverished black and Hispanic people living in urban ghettos. Inner-city ghetto conditions provide both the motive and opportunity for violent criminal behavior and the growth of these ghettos coincides with the rise in urban crime rates.

The FBI's Uniform Crime Reports show that blacks, who constitute 11 percent of the population, account for about 43 percent of all criminal offenders arrested for violent crimes. In two crucial categories of such crimes—homicides and robberies—black offenders actually outnumber whites on a nation-wide basis, rural and urban areas included. But the disproportion is much larger in the cities where the incidence and fear of violent crime is greatest. A study of arrests in seventeen large American cities located in every region of the country, conducted under the auspices of the President's Commission on the Causes of Crime and Prevention of Violence, indicated that the "race of the offenders" was black in 72 percent of criminal homicides, 74 percent of aggravated assaults, 81 percent of unarmed robberies, and a whopping 85 percent of armed robberies.

But do studies based on police department records reflect the actual proportion of black offenders or merely a pervasive bias against offenders who are black? According to some scholars the entire difference in the arrest rates of whites and blacks may simply mean that when blacks commit a crime the victims are more likely to call the police and the police are more likely to respond, find the offenders, and place them under arrest. With the introduction of the Crime Victimization surveys, I think this interpretation has lost much of its credibility. Comparisons of crime data from the FBI with the victimization studies indicate that the disproportion between white and black crime rates may be inflated at most by about 10 percent for assaults and rapes. But for robberies, the two sets of data converge. (Homicides, as indicated earlier, cannot be studied by the victimization reports.) Conservatively speaking, about 62 percent of all robbery offenders are black. Proportionate to their representation in the total population, blacks are therefore fourteen times more likely than whites to commit a robbery offense!

This means that much of the glaring discrepancy between United States crime rates and the crime rates of other countries can be traced to the disproportionate share of violent crimes committed by blacks. Minus crimes committed by blacks, America's rates of violent crime are much closer to the rates found in other countries. For example, while the national robbery rate is eight times higher than England's, the white robbery rate is only three times higher. Similarly, although the overall homicide rate in the United States is five times higher than Japan's, the white homicide rate is only twice as high.

True, this still leaves substantial differences, but the white crime rate is based on data which classifies Hispanics as white. In many U.S. cities Hispanics constitute an ethnic underclass with rising crime rates and the same motivations and opportunities for violent crime as one finds among blacks. Subtracting the Hispanic crime rate from the rest of the white crime rate would further reduce the difference between crime rates in the United States and those found in Japan and Britain, neither of which has an equally large racial or ethnic underclass living under conditions comparable to those found in America's inner cities. (Moreover, the recent increase in crime rates in Great Britain parallels the growth of racial and ethnic ghettos inhabited by immigrants from India and the West Indies.)

The argument has now reached the point where it is necessary to explain the high rate of criminal violence among blacks and, to a lesser degree, Hispanics. Not race but hopeless poverty and chronic unemployment provide the key. During and after World War II, U.S. blacks migrated in unprecedented numbers from farms to cities in search of factory jobs. What they found instead was an economy in rapid transition from goods production to service-and-information production. Today over half of America's blacks live in major cities, and over half of these—about seven and one-half million people —live in the dirtiest and most dilapidated inner cores of these cities. During the 1970s, while the number of large-central-city whites living in poverty declined by 5 percent, the number of large-central-city blacks living in poverty increased by 21 percent.

Officially, the unemployment rate for blacks stands at about 12 percent. But this figure includes only people who are actively looking for work. It does not include blacks who have part-time jobs but who want full-time jobs; nor does it include those who have stopped looking for work because they could not find anything acceptable. Adding the hidden unemployed to the officially unemployed raises the rate to 25 percent (compared to 12 percent for whites calculated on the same basis). But that is still only the tip of the iceberg. Ronald H. Brown of the National Urban League calculates that over half of all black teenagers are unemployed; and in ghettos like Harlem the rate among young blacks may be as high as 86 percent.

It is my contention that hundreds of thousands of unemployed blacks choose violent crime as a solution to the chronic despair and envy that they must otherwise endure—especially young black men for whom failure looms as condemnation of manhood as well as a sentence to perpetual want.

I have to take note of a body of scholarly opinion which claims that poverty in general has little to do with the high rate of criminal violence in the United States and therefore that black unemployment and poverty are not sufficient in themselves to account for the extraordinarily high rates of black crime. True enough, if one simply compares crime rates by states or cities, those with low per capita incomes do not necessarily have high rates of criminal violence. But the poverty of the black ghetto is different from the poverty of rural whites or of an earlier generation of urban ethnics. Unlike the rural poor, inner-city blacks have the opportunity as well as the motive to commit violent crimes. The city is an ideal setting for finding and surprising one's victims and successfully eluding the police. One can scarcely mug a farmer in a cornfield and expect to get away with it. Also, unlike the European immigrants of previous generations, with the passage of time blacks have become more and not less concentrated inside their ghettos. The lesson of the four decades since 1940 is that only a tiny percentage of blacks born in the inner cities will ever earn enough money to participate in the American dream.

Under these conditions, the benefits of criminal behavior

easily outweigh the risks of getting caught and being sent to jail. John Conyers, himself a member of the black congressional caucus, writes: "When survival is at stake, it should not be surprising that criminal activity begins to resemble an opportunity rather than a cost, work rather than deviance, and a possibly profitable undertaking that is superior to a coerced existence directed by welfare bureaucrats." For many black youths there is no opposition between crime and a career. Crime *is* their career. That is the main reason, it seems to me, why 70 percent of blacks who have gone to jail once will go to jail at least once again.

The muggers who have turned America's inner-city streets into no-man's lands are not in the main pathological degenerates born with a lust for violence and criminality. Mugging is their profession! Sociologist Robert Lejeune found that the typical inexperienced mugger was as terrified as the victim. But after a few attacks, muggers begin to manage if not to eliminate their fear.

One mugger recounted how he had felt progressively better with each mugging until he could just go up to a "dude" and say, "Give me your money." Others explained that mugging soon become a matter-of-fact, "normal" part of their lives: "I don't have any money. Well, eh, that guy looks good. Let's get him." Muggers learn to identify targets who have some money and who won't give them too much trouble. (Lejeune's muggers did not discuss the fact that many if not most victims are women and helpless old people.) One mugger boasted that his trade had become so easy that he could count on getting money on Friday as if it were a regular payday.

From the victim's point of view, muggers seem to use force in a capricious fashion, but the muggers themselves claim to be following certain professional guidelines, adjusting their mode of attack to their perception of the victim's strength and courage. Whether it be a rationalization or not, muggers insist that violence is something most victims bring down on themselves as a result of interfering with the muggers' way of making a living. Explaining why he became violent when a "dude"

126

didn't cooperate and hand over his wallet, one mugger said, "I felt like it was my right; it was my due."

Several studies have shown that for the nation as a whole crime rates tend to move up and down with unemployment rates. In an appearance before the House of Representatives Subcommittee on Crime, Johns Hopkins Professor Harvey M. Brenner testified that every one percent increase in the overall unemployment rate results in a 6 percent increase in the number of robberies and a 4 percent increase in the number of homicides. While Brenner's work is important for proving the causal connection between unemployment and crime, the post-World War II increase in violent crimes cannot be entirely accounted for by his method. Unemployment among inner-city black males has always been high, especially during periods of recession. The percent of unemployed black males has not changed so drastically since World War II. What has changed is that practically all of the unemployed blacks are now concentrated in the cities. Where earlier 25 percent black unemployed meant two or three hundred thousand desperate men living in blighted ghettos, today the same percentage means two or three million.

Older Americans who fondly recall being able to sleep in the city parks during hot summer evenings and feeling at ease while using public transport and walking city streets late at night are not exaggerating the contrast between then and now. Even during the Great Depression, parks, streets, subways, and buses (or streetcars) were far safer than they are today. Why? Because unemployed blacks as yet constituted only a small percentage of the population of the biggest cities. Most of the urban unemployed were whites, who believed that there was "a rainbow in the sky just around the corner" and that they would soon be going back to work at good jobs. Today, unemployed inner city blacks know from bitter experience that there is no rainbow in the sky for them. The choice of crime as a career is no spur-of-the-moment thing. It takes years of chronic unemployment and hopelessness.

If the argument up to now is correct and it is black unemployment that accounts for most of the great post-World War II crime wave in America's cities, then the next question to be answered is why blacks remain chronically unemployed. But before I try to answer this question and show how black unemployment relates to the changing nature of work and the composition of the U.S. labor force, let me make some cautionary remarks. Liberal sociologists and criminologists expend a considerable amount of effort trying to disprove or play down the connection between race and crime. In order not to fan the flames of racial bigotry, some newspapers and wire services have even dropped all mention of a criminal's racial identity from their news stories. Like the earlier ban on gathering census data and labor statistics separately for blacks and whites, these efforts are well-intentioned but self-defeating. To play down the black (or Hispanic) contribution to violent crime is to mask the true price that America is paying for its racism, chronic unemployment, and inner-city decay.

In bringing the facts about black crime rates into the open, one should also note that blacks themselves proportionately suffer more from violent crimes than do whites. Poor blacks for example are twenty-five times more likely than wealthy whites to be a victim of a robbery resulting in injury, and the ratio of black homicide victims to white homicide victims is eight to one. In fact, homicide is the ranking killer of black males between fifteen and twenty-four years of age. More black males die from homicide than from motor vehicle accidents, diabetes, emphysema, or pneumonia. Two out of five black male children born in an American city will not reach age twenty-five. Now, on to the question of why it has been so difficult to reduce black unemployment.

While many experts agree that there is a connection between chronic unemployment among inner-city black males and high crime rates, the reason for high black male unemployment rates is still widely misunderstood. Some people place the blame for not finding jobs on black men themselves. They think the jobs are there but that black men don't want them.

128

But as anthropologist Elliot Liebow discovered in his classic study of black street-corner men in Washington, D.C.: "The most important fact is that a man who is able and willing to work cannot earn enough money to support himself, his wife and one or more children. A man's chances for working regularly are good only if he is willing to work for less than he can live on, and sometimes not even then."

Recently, much confusion has been generated by the idea that black unemployment is the fault of the black family rather than of the structure of the labor market. Black inner-city families, it is said, are unstable since a high percentage of them are headed by women and there are no husbands present. In cities like Chicago and Washington, D.C., over half of the total births of black women are out-of-wedlock. The black male child therefore grows up without having a father who holds a steady job. Lacking a proper "role model," black youths drop out of school and follow a career of delinquency and crime. Daniel Moynihan used this line of reasoning to reach his controversial conclusion that the way to solve the problems of the inner cities was to concentrate on building stable home lives for ghetto youngsters.

The trouble with this idea is that it does not tell us why inner-city black women are less likely than whites to marry and live with the fathers of their children. It is true that a disproportionate share of mother-centered, "fatherless" families are black. But do blacks have such high unemployment rates because they have so many fatherless families or do they have so many fatherless families because they have such high unemployment rates? In my view it is unemployment that causes the fatherless family, not the fatherless family that causes unemployment.

Numerous anthropological studies have shown that mother-centered, father-absent families occur wherever men have trouble finding steady jobs and women can earn as much as or more than men. If men are frequently out of work, and make too little to support a family when they do work, it does not pay for a woman who has an income of her own to commit herself permanently in marriage to one man. She is better off keeping her options open and accepting male consorts in temporary liaisons, letting them live with her when they can make supplementary contributions to the household, and putting them out of the house when they become a burden.

But this seems to lead to another conundrum: Why do inner-city black women continue to have babies under such adverse circumstances? Why should the out-of-wedlock rate among black women be six times greater than among white women? If we apply the theory that relates declining fertility to the costs and benefits of rearing children in cities as set forth earlier in this book, it appears at first sight that there is no rational explanation for the out-of-wedlock birth rate and the incidence of mother-centered black families remaining so high. Consequently, many people assume that there is something in the racial or cultural heritage of blacks that inclines them to have illegitimate children and form mother-centered households. Some anthropologists used to claim that mother-centered families among blacks were a "survival" of African cultural traditions, while historians and sociologists argued that slavery, not cultural tradition, was responsible because slave owners separated husbands from wives and encouraged promiscuity. Recent studies tend to refute both of these earlier views. The mother-centered inner-city black family is neither an African tradition nor a product of slavery. Historian Herbert Gutman has shown that two-parent families actually predominated among American blacks during the period of slavery and that stable two-parent black families were the rule both in rural and urban communities after the Civil War. In the countryside, black farm families were once no more mother-centered than white farm families. While in the cities, black fathers working as mechanics, house painters, carpenters, plumbers, and at other crafts earned enough to maintain stable male breadwinner families. It was only after the great wave of European immigration when urban black males were forced out of these jobs by racist hiring practices that the pattern of mother-centeredness began to develop.

What then is the explanation for the fact that the number of families headed by black single women rose 257 percent in the 1970s while the number of their out-of-wedlock births rose by 50 percent? The answer I believe lies in the peculiarities of the U.S. welfare system rather than in any supposed racial or cultural peculiarities of people of African descent. Not welfare in general but the extraordinary federal program known as Aid to Families with Dependent Children or AFDC for short. Since the end of World War II this program has played a crucial role not only in shaping the organization of the black family but in shaping the entire pattern of inner-city life as well. One might even say that through AFDC, the federal government places its stamp of approval on both the fatherless inner-city family and the pursuit of crime as the solution to black men's unemployment problems. Let me explain.

Budgeted at about eleven billion dollars a year, AFDC is the largest of the government's welfare programs for able-bodied people living in the inner cities. Its principal stated objective is "to maintain and strengthen family life." Over half of the three and a half million families receiving AFDC benefits in the form of housing allowances and cash stipends are black or Hispanic.

AFDC has been craftily engineered by politicians and welfare experts to prevent it from becoming a guaranteed income plan for able-bodied families headed by chronically unemployed parents. Such a plan is feared because it would act as a disincentive for able-bodied Americans to look for work. The first intended safeguard against AFDC becoming a permanent family dole is the famous no-man-in-the-house rule. Ninety-six percent of the AFDC caseload consists of fatherless families. If a child's father moves in with the family, payments cease, on the assumption that the man should fulfill his breadwinner responsibilities. If any other man moves in with the family and sleeps with the mother, payments cease on the assumption that the government would then be subsidizing immoral behavior and would not be maintaining and strengthening family life. Theoretically, the no-man-in-the-house rule should discourage women and men from using AFDC as a means of having sex and raising children at government expense.

The second safeguard against AFDC becoming a permanent substitute for wages earned at work is that AFDC benefits are set below poverty-level incomes. The AFDC mother gets a stipend for herself and each child plus an allowance for housing costs. In addition most AFDC families automatically receive benefits in the form of food stamps. Counting food stamps but not the housing allowance, an AFDC family of four in a high benefit state will have a maximum disposable income of about $4,250 in 1980 dollars. Of this sum, $3,500 will be needed to satisfy a "no frills" minimum standard of nutrition, leaving only $750 in cash for all other nonmedical expenses including utilities, clothing, school supplies, toys, transportation, furniture, movies, blankets, soap, toothpaste, and other personal items for an entire year.

Despite the humiliating and punitive no-man-in-the-house rule and despite the meager cash benefits, the number of inner-city women on or seeking to get on AFDC has increased steadily. If anything, AFDC seems to have encouraged rather than discouraged the development of inner-city female-headed families living on the dole. Why? Wouldn't these women be better off if they practiced strict birth control, never got pregnant, and stayed off AFDC?

Not necessarily. AFDC with all of its penalties and humiliations looms as the best of a lot of bad bargains. Opting for a career as an AFDC mother provides inner-city women with an income that is at least sufficient for renting an apartment. This not only assures them that they will have a place to live, but it gives them a considerable amount of leverage in interpersonal affairs, especially with inner-city men who often lack a place to sleep. Since AFDC women are automatically entitled to medicaid, free medical care is an additional inducement for getting on AFDC (although I would not want to include for-gone medical bills in calculating AFDC family income the way some economists do as proof that AFDC benefits are set too high—families cannot eat a paid doctor's bill). In a world without stability and assets, AFDC therefore is a kind of nest egg, a vital resource that puts women and motherhood at the center of things. Inner-city men respect women who have this re-source; they vie with each other for their favors. And by hav-ing children with them the men establish a claim on the shelter which women control. As anthropologist Carol Stack has shown in her study of a black Midwestern ghetto neighbor-hood, AFDC women have a surprisingly large circle of rela-tives based on ties built up by their sequential liaisons. These kinship ties give AFDC women additional security and influ-ence and people to turn to in case of emergencies.

But the decisive factor in the cost/benefit balance of AFDC motherhood is the unenforceability of the no-man-in-the-house rule. If AFDC women had to rely on the official legal stipend for maintaining themselves and their children, I think they would soon get out of the welfare baby business. But as every social worker knows, almost all inner-city AFDC women count on supplementary incomes from husbands-in-hiding, co-resident male consorts, or former consort fathers of their chil-dren. Enter the crime connection.

In a unique study, anthropologist Jagna Sharff found that all the mothers in a group of twenty-four Hispanic AFDC families living in New York City's Lower East Side had some kind of male consort. While few of the men-in-the-house held regular full-time jobs, even those who were unemployed chipped in something toward food and rent from selling stolen goods, dealing in marijuana or cocaine, and from an occasional bur-glary or mugging. Some women had more than one consort while others picked up money and gifts through relationships that were hard to distinguish from prostitution.

Another factor in the benefit column of AFDC motherhood

is that the budget for inner-city household expenditures goes further than the reported income would seem to indicate. Inner-city AFDC children are adept at shoplifting and there are many bargains available to AFDC families as a result of the circulation of stolen goods. Moreover, unlike middle-class children, inner-city children begin to have incomes of their own at an early age and cease to be a burden to their mothers by their late teens. In their early teens young inner-city boys can make substantial contributions to the household's economic balance through their involvement in street crimes and dope peddling. In addition, they confer an important benefit upon their mothers in the form of protection against the risk of rapes, muggings, and various kinds of rip-offs to which ghetto families are perpetually exposed.

Sharff found that AFDC mothers value sons for streetwise, *macho* qualities, especially their ability to use knives or guns, which are needed to protect the family against unruly or predatory neighbors. While the AFDC mothers did not actively encourage their sons to enter the drug trade, everyone recognized that a successful drug dealer could become a very rich man. To get ahead in the drug business one needs the same *macho* qualities that are useful in defending one's family. When a young man brings home his first drug profits, mothers have mixed feelings of pride and apprehension. Since young ghetto males have a 40 percent chance of dying by age twenty-five, a ghetto mother has to have more than one son if she hopes to enjoy the protection of a streetwise male. In her sample of AFDC families, Sharff compiled this record of male homicides in the three-year period 1976 to 1979:

Victim's Age	Immediate Cause of Death
25	Shot in drug-related incident
19	Shot in dispute in grocery store
21	Shot in drug-related incident
28	Stabbed in drug-related incident
32	"Suicide" in a police precinct house

30	Stabbed in drug-related incident
28	Poisoned by adulterated heroin
30	Arson victim
24	Shot in drug-related incident
19	Tortured and stabbed in drug-related incident

AFDC girls have their contributions to make also. Not being overly concerned with regular school attendance they can baby-sit for the younger children, shop, and clean house. And at sixteen they can get pregnant and apply for AFDC on their own, adding their own child's stipend to the family's income and perpetuating the female-centered "dynasty" of their mother and grandmothers. And so, despite all the crafty scheming that has gone into the design of AFDC, the program has succeeded best in achieving exactly what it was designed to prevent: the formation of mother-centered families living on the dole who make up for their welfare deficits by tolerating or encouraging adult and juvenile crime.

One must be careful not to conclude that every family on AFDC conforms to the pattern described by Sharff. For some mothers, AFDC merely represents a one-time emergency source of funds used in the aftermath of divorce or separation until they can find a job and arrange for child care. But several million inner-city women, mostly black and Hispanic, use AFDC not as a temporary crutch but as a regular or recurrent source of subsistence. A hard core of such women—estimated by sociologists Martin Rein and Lee Rainwater to number about 750,000—stay on AFDC for as many as twelve years at a stretch. And a far larger number of inner-city women follow a pattern of going on and off AFDC as they move in and out of the labor market between pregnancies.

I think I have now shown that it is not inner-city mother-centered families that cause unemployment, welfare dependency and inner-city crime, but that it is unemployment and welfare dependency that cause inner-city mother-centered families and the crime that goes with them. But I have yet to answer the question of why inner-city male unemployment rates remain so high.

From the holistic point of view of this book, the most important point bearing on crime and unemployment among black males is that during and after World War II blacks migrated in unprecedented numbers from farms to cities in search of union-wage factory jobs. This was scarcely a voluntary movement since it coincided with the end of the epoch of small farms and with the final stages of the industrialization of agriculture. But it was precisely during this same period that the great shift from goods production to service-and-information production was taking place. This resulted in a massive pile-up of unemployed black workers inside the run-down cores of the nation's largest cities.

Why wasn't this great army of unskilled workers called upon to take part in the explosive expansion of the new information-and-people-processing economy? Because, as we already know, the growth of the service economy coincided with—was predicated upon—the mass conversion of the reserve army of white housewives from baby production and services in the home to the production of services and information away from home. The fact that white women were preferred over black men in the only sector of the job market that has been expanding during the last forty years accounts, I think, for the uniquely grim prospects of the black and Hispanic underclass in the United States as compared with the experiences of European ethnics earlier in the century. All the affirmative-action, Head Start, and CETA programs in the world cannot compensate for the depressing effect on black male prospects of the explosive entrance of cheap white female service-and-information workers into the labor market. White women seeking employment in the service sector enjoy a decisive competitive edge over black males. Far more of them have high school and college degrees; they speak standard English instead of black English, and they have fewer hang-ups about working in a subordinate position with respect to white male bosses and supervisors. While white male employers may be prejudiced against hiring women, they are far more prejudiced against hiring black men. The disastrous consequences for black males of the white housewife's rush into service-and-information jobs shows up plainly in the statistics on employment in the private sector of the economy. As the number of white women holding private sector jobs increases, black men are being driven out and are coming to depend more and more on the government to hire them or are joining the ranks of the unemployed. Between 1974 and 1977, while the proportion of new jobs acquired by white women in the private sector increased by 72 percent, the proportion acquired by black men decreased by 11 percent.

As white women intensify their struggle to achieve parity with males at all levels of the workforce, they are not only dimming the prospects for black males to find dead-end jobs as clerks, secretaries, hot dog vendors, and filling station attendants, but they are rapidly eroding the gains made by black men during the 1960s in good jobs at middle management levels. Affirmative action consultant Robert Goldfarb reports that corporations have recently swung toward favoring the promotion of white women to a far greater extent than black men. Employers "are more comfortable advancing white women," "devote more attention and effort to recruiting and training women," and are "impatient with black subordinates." As a sop toward fulfilling government affirmative-action requirements, most employers would now rather advance a young white woman with a degree from an ivy league college than an older black man with a shaky educational background and a chip on his shoulder.

Searching for ways to attain affirmative-action goals despite their mounting frustration, some white male executives intensified their recruiting and training of white women. The same men who until recently ignored or blunted the advancement of women began to see in them an opportunity to reach hiring goals without having to deal with black men. Burning with ambition, women seized this support. As a result, black men feel squeezed out in this competition for a diminishing number of opportunities for promotion, training and jobs.

One of the most devastating effects of the expansion in the number of white working wives is the decrease in the percentage of black families in which both husband and wife hold jobs. Before the era of women's liberation, proportionately more black families than white families enjoyed two incomes (not of course because black women were "liberated," but because their husbands' wages were so low). But since 1967, according to Robert Hill, director of research of the National Urban League, "The surge in the labor force participation of white women has resulted in white families, for the first time, having a higher percent (55%) of multiple earners than black families (46%)." This has resulted not only in a widening gap between white and black family incomes, but a further increase in the proportion of black inner-city families headed by women. For as black males leave the labor force, women no longer value them as potential husbands or fathers; and at the same time the men themselves cease to value marriage as a feasible or desirable goal. Single-parent, female-centered families are in no sense aberrant or pathological, but the undeniable fact is that such families tend to be twice as poor as two-parent families. Unwittingly therefore, white women, responding to their own economic imperative clothed in the rhetoric of sexual liberation, are steadily tightening the vise that holds the ghetto in its jaws. And to the extent that inner-city poverty figures in the silent calculus that beckons black youth to a career in crime, to that extent women's liberation has been their silent partner.

Some will object that the rise in white female job seekers has no place in the causal web linking blacks to escalating crime rates, since the kinds of jobs taken by white women have for the most part been jobs that inner-city black men would not or could not have taken anyway. While this may hold true for secretarial and typing positions, it is not true of millions of jobs in public administration and the retail trades, nor of bookkeepers, cashiers, clerks and tellers, receptionists, schoolteachers, and dental and medical assistants. By responding to the call-up for these jobs, white women cut the ground out from any possibility of a large-scale call-up of unemployed black males. For with employment in the manufacturing sector on the decline there was no other part of the economy to which black youth could conceivably have turned.

The further objection that white women had nothing to do with the black male's high dropout rate and functional illiteracy also misses the mark. The lack of interest exhibited by black males in acquiring the educational prerequisites for white-collar service jobs, and the de facto corresponding lack of interest on the part of the educational establishment in heading black students in the direction of white-collar careers, has a great deal to do with the prior availability of an abundance of properly credentialed white women eager to step into every new opening. If these women had stayed home, the demand for service-and-information workers might have translated itself into the development of a white-collar career orientation for black males and into an upgrading of the teaching of basic white-collar skills in black ghetto schools. It was precisely because there was no demand in the white-collar service sector for literate black males that acquiring a high school diploma has always seemed like such a futile exercise for all concerned.

I suppose that these remarks will be misconstrued and that I shall be accused of saying that white women are the cause of black unemployment. Of course, I intend nothing of the sort. United States unemployment is a structural problem related to technological change, the growth of oligopolies, and the continuous substitution of machines for labor. Women are not responsible for the changes in the economy that put blacks at a disadvantage. Both women and blacks are equally victims, but in different ways, of inflation. No, the point I want to make

139

is simply that America's problems cannot be understood piecemeal. It is not enough for us to raise our consciousness concerning women's plight as unpaid housewives and underpaid secretaries. While helping women to find equal opportunity in the labor force, must we not also raise our consciousness about the men who are at the bottom of the heap? For without solving the problem of the black and Hispanic underclass, I don't see how there can be a women's liberation in the United States—unless one considers a life spent behind locked doors and barred windows in fear of being mugged and raped a form of liberation.

8

Why
the Cults
Are Coming

The major aspect of America's cultural crisis that remains to be brought into our holistic framework is religion. Along with shoddy goods and services, the disintegration of the family, libertine sex, and the great post-World War II crime wave, have come startling new forms of religious beliefs and practices. This can scarcely be a mere coincidence. But the precise nature of the relationship between religion and the other elements of change is a controversial matter. Can religion be brought into the causal web that accounts for the other changes discussed so far? Yes, but only if we are willing to take a rational and objective view of what the new religious consciousness is all about. I hope to show that much of the current spiritual thrust not only reflects widespread bewilderment and frustration with problems such as crime, unemployment, disservices, misinformation, oligopoly, and bureaucracy, but that it also constitutes a misunderstood attempt to save America's dream of worldly progress by magical and supernatural means.

In the 1960s theologians despairingly pondered the question of whether God was dead. By the 1970s, the United States was teeming with people claiming to have seen God alive, or to be living gods themselves. America's religious awakening involves more than a reaffirmed belief in an active, personal deity. The forms of awakening range from weekend encounter groups to murderous messianic prophets. No single term such as spiritual or religious properly characterizes the whole spectrum of this renaissance. As Theodore Roszak, one of the proponents of the new "religious consciousness" rightly suggests, we would have to concoct an unusable word such as "psycho-mystico-parascientific-spiritual-therapeutic" to do justice to the broad scope of all the new sects, movements, therapies, cults, and churches that began to appear toward the end of the 1960s. It would take a small telephone book just to list all the Swamis, Gurus, Sris, Bubas, Babas, Bawas, Yogis, Yogas, Maharishis, and Maharajis who began to find disciples in America, not to mention all the Jesus freaks, encounter groups, UFO cults, and the rest.

Once again there is the interesting question of timing. Cults and movements arose in clusters at about the same time that many of the other changes discussed in this book were taking place.

For example, the Children of God, one of the first Jesus freak movements, appeared in California in 1968. "Hare Krishna" started in New York in 1964. Transcendental meditation began to flourish in the late 1960s. Scientology, which had started out as a form of secular therapy in the 1950s called Dianetics, went into eclipse and then entered a period of rapid growth as a religion at the end of the 1960s. The First Unification Church followers of Reverend Sun Myung Moon arrived in America in 1959 but it was not until 1971 that the "Moonies" began to spread. Maharaj Ji's Divine Light Mission was planted in America in 1971. Healthy, Happy, Holy, an offshoot of Indian Sikhism, appeared in 1968.

"All of these groups became visible and began to grow rapidly in the four or five year period bridging the 1960's and 1970's."

Since all the other aspects of the American way of life were in flux, it is not surprising that religious beliefs and practices also began to change during this period. The experience of other cultures and historical epochs demonstrates that stresses brought on by rapid cultural change usually find expression in spiritual yearning, questing, and experimenting which leads to an expansion and intensification of religious activity, broadly defined.

All of the major world religions were born during times of rapid cultural transformations. Buddhism and Hinduism arose in the Ganges Valley of Northern India during an epoch of deforestation, population increase, and state formation. Judaism arose during prolonged migrations of the ancient Israelites. Christianity arose in conjunction with attempts to break the yoke of Roman imperialism. Islam arose during the transition from a life of pastoral nomadism to that of trade and empires in Arabia and North Africa. Protestants split from Catholicism as feudalism gave way to capitalism. Messianic and millenarian cults swept across the Great Plains as the American Indians lost their lands and hunting grounds. And in the wake of the European colonization of New Guinea and Melanesia, hundreds of "cargo cults," devoted to acquiring worldly wealth with the assistance of ancestors returned from the dead, spread from island to island.

At least twice before in the history of the United States, periods of rapid social and economic change have given birth to an upwelling of religious and spiritual ferment. Historians call these periods "Great Awakenings." The first "Great Awakening" occurred in the years preceding the American Revolution, while the second occurred in the years preceding the Civil War. The present-day religious renaissance is already being called the "Third Great Awakening."

There is a widespread but I think erroneous notion that the new religious consciousness is primarily a reaction to Western materialism. As seen by Berkeley sociologist Robert Bellah for example, the most representative aspect of the Third Great

Awakening is the acceptance of "Asian spirituality" as an antidote for Western "utilitarian individualism." Unlike traditional Western religions, Bellah argues, Asian religions emphasize inner experience over external achievement, harmony with nature over exploitation of nature, and intense personal relations with a guru over impersonal relations with ministers and priests. According to Bellah, aspects of Zen, Taoism, Buddhism, Hinduism, Sufism, and other oriental religions first began to strike a responsive chord in the "counter-culture" of the late sixties as Americans began to feel that the struggle to achieve material gains by and for individuals was hollow and meaningless. Helped along by drugs and meditation, the counter-culture generation realized the "illusoriness of worldly striving."

> Careerism and status-seeking, the sacrifice of present fulfillment for some ever-receding future goal, no longer seemed worthwhile.

Asian religion supposedly provided a critique of "the continuous expansion of wealth and power" and was responsive to the questioning of "whether the quality of life was a simple function of wealth and power, or whether the endless accumulation of wealth and power was not destroying the quality and meaning of life." Recognizing that the United States had many unsolved material problems such as racism and poverty, Bellah nonetheless insists that the crisis was brought on as much by "the success of the society" and by the "realization that education and affluence did not bring happiness or fulfillment" as by its failures. Following this line of reasoning to its logical outcome, we are led to conclude that the basic cause of the Third Great Awakening is a crisis of spirit and meaning rather than a crisis of practical material needs. Writes Bellah:

> The deepest cause, no matter what particular factors contributed to the actual timing, was, in my opinion, the inability of utilitarian individualism to provide a meaningful pattern of personal and so-

144

cial existence. . . . I would thus interpret the crisis of the sixties above all as a crisis of meaning, a religious crisis.

This theory, if I have represented it fairly, runs counter to the main thrust of my own interpretation of the current cultural crisis. Of course, everyone agrees that people are searching for new ultimate meanings to replace those lost or damaged during the 1960s. But can America's spiritual and religious questing be attributed in whole or in part to material *success?* Only if one believes that America in the sixties was an affluent society. But, as was shown in previous chapters, much of the post-World War II rise in living standards was illusory. The quantity of goods and services increased but the quality declined. Married women were not pushed or pulled into the labor force by spiritual questing but by unpaid bills. The breadwinner family and the marital and procreative imperative were not destroyed by affluence but by an inability to reconcile the costs of child-rearing with the maintenance of middle-class standards of consumption. Was it a quest for ultimate meaning that caused the dollar to shrink, put millions out of work and on the dole, and turned America's cities into crime-ridden combat zones?

It seems to me more plausible that the deepest and most characteristic impulse of the Third Great Awakening is not the search for ultimate meaning but the search for solutions to America's unsolved economic and social problems. The human quest for ultimate meaning is a formidable force in history, but it rarely if ever exists apart from, above, beyond, or in opposition to the quest for solutions to practical problems.

It seems to me that the role of "Asiatic" spirituality in the formation and propagation of new religious groups and rituals in the United States has been exaggerated. The number of people involved in new cults, sects, and movements which have contemplation, withdrawal from worldly affairs, and other supposedly "Asiatic" motifs as their principal concern, is actually quite small by comparison with the number involved in cults and sects and movements which have a definite program for mastering worldly problems and enhancing individual material welfare.

The point seems rather self-evident for those Americans who want to predict the future from horoscopes, cure illness through shamanic trances, or disable their boss or teacher by sticking pins in dolls. These are all techniques for mastering the world rather than for retreating from it. Like all good shamans, Don Juan, the mythical hero of Carlos Castaneda's multivolume paean to sorcery, uses his knowledge of "non-ordinary" reality mainly to gain power over his enemies.

That Americans are now resorting to magical formulas and shamanic states of consciousness to predict and influence the course of events is an intelligible reaction to the disappointing consequences of such scientific miracles as high-compression automobile engines, nuclear power, and computerized billing systems. If people get thirsty enough, they will try to squeeze water out of a stone. Perhaps this is putting it too harshly. If scientific technology is costly and known to be counterproductive, and magical technology is cheap, one might as well try magic even if the expectation of success is not very great.

Utilitarian motives are also self-evident in the seemingly endless varieties of weekend encounter groups and mind-body therapies that are part of the "human-potential movement." Executives prescribe encounter groups and sensitivity training courses to improve relationships among employees and to step up sales. "Rolfing," a painful form of skeletal "realignment," releases body tensions so that people can experience "greater physical freedom and balance." Arica exercises "dramatically improve the quality of personal life" and bring "the individual a more elastic energized body and a clearer mind." Bioenergetics promises to make people more effective, creative, imaginative.

In the more "etherealized" and spiritualized "trainings,"

the predominant, recurring theme is that of mind over matter. Not only do participants expect to control others by improving their control over themselves but they expect to control physical happenings by the imposition of their thoughts on matter. Erhard Seminars Training ("est"), for example, claims that thought is the basic stuff out of which the universe is constructed. Learning how to take responsibility for one's thoughts and to impose them on events therefore can lead to the kind of worldly success that est's founder, Werner Erhard, enjoys. "If you really understand self-responsibility," said one est graduate, "it means that nobody has to die unless he chooses to; all deaths are suicides, and there are no accidents. And you can fly if you allow yourself to know how." Similar extreme forms of mentalism—belief in the omnipotence of thought—characterize the principles and goals of many of the more "meditative" human-potential disciplines.

After learning Transcendental Meditation ("TM") as taught by Maharishi Mahesh Yogi, "an individual naturally engages in activity more effectively without accumulating stress and strain." Silva Mind Control promises "improved productivity, ability to solve problems, habit control, better memory, health, extra-sensory perception, and increased vitality."

Several "trainings" and therapies have evolved into full-fledged organized religions without losing their essentially practical and worldly orientations. Scientology, which began as a psychotherapy called Dianetics, typifies the manipulative and power-hungry side of the new consciousness. Although Scientology's theories are heavily "spiritualized," the course which leads to a knowledge of these theories has a bottom line frankly rooted in practical affairs.

Ron Hubbard, the founder of Scientology, holds that each individual has a true self or "thetan," an immortal, omniscient, and omnipotent entity similar to souls or gods in conventional Judeo-Christian theology. Thetans created the material aspects of the world and the "game of life" in order to amuse themselves. But they became so involved in the material universe which they had created—matter, energy, space, and time—that they forgot their origins and lost their ability to use their spiritual powers. To recover the use of these spiritual powers, Scientologists take a series of courses, designed to clear away repressed and forgotten memories of incidents that are responsible for the loss of Thetan powers. People who have not taken the training courses are called "pre-clears." As the Scientologists move upward through various levels of training, they aspire to reach the state of being known as "clear." Ultimately they hope to become "operating Thetans" at which point they will have regained many of their lost powers.

In obligatory testimonials collected by the church's "Success Department," Clears and Operating Thetans cite worldly achievements such as "not worrying and bogging myself down with a burden of problems"; "freedom from my compulsions"; "I no longer feel afraid of anything"; "ability to change body size"; "ability to see through walls"; and "ability to hear other people's thoughts."

In a world full of machines that don't work, Operating Thetan Vicki Dickey's testimonial has special import:

> Today was fantastic. I walked downstairs to get some coffee and the coffee machine was buzzing. So I put my hands out and moved them around the machine putting out beams to bounce back and thereby I would tell by watching the particles flow exactly where the error in the machine was. I found it and corrected the molecular structure of that area in the machine and the buzzing stopped. Then I heard my air conditioner rattling so I looked at why it was rattling and it stopped.

If anything, Scientologists prefer to exaggerate rather than minimize the movement's access to wealth and power. Ron Hubbard's personal wealth—he travels about the globe in a fleet of ocean-going ships—is a great inspiration to preclears. "We own quite a bit of property over the world," Hubbard boasts. "We will be acquiring more, as well as some countries." "Money is a symbol," Hubbard once said. "It represents success when you have it and defeat when you don't, no matter who is putting out propaganda to the contrary."

It is true that many of the better-known and more controversial communitarian "cults" represent themselves as being opposed to the materialism and consumerism of American society. On joining the "Moonies," the "Hare Krishnas," or the Divine Light Mission, new members are expected to turn over all or most of their cash and valuables to the movement. For the ordinary cult member, life in the communal houses, temples, or "ashrams" is spartan. They must subsist on cheap vegetarian fare and they must refrain from premarital or extramarital sex. Devotees spend long hours in prayer, meditation, and chanting. Yet each of these cults has a definite worldly commitment—a yearning for control—which contradicts the notion that the current religious awakening is best understood as an Asian-inspired "critique of the expansion of wealth and power."

A former Moonie, Alan Tate Wood, for example explains that Reverend Moon's final victory can come about in two ways: through ideological battle or through physical force. "What was settled ideologically would be settled peacefully. But those who did not come along willingly would be scourged with the worldly arsenal of napalm and nukes." To create the "material base" for the impending battle, the Moonies own and operate several factories in Korea, one of which manufactures rifles. They maintain a corps of lobbyists in Washington and engage in an aggressive program of real estate purchases. Members view the expansion of the cult's factories, stores, and real estate holdings as evidence of a favorable tide in the cosmic struggle. The need to create the material base for the spiritual war dominates the actual daily life of the Moonie communes. Moonies spend far more time recruiting, panhandling, and selling than meditating or praying. The bulk of Moon's income comes from the sale of flowers, candles, and candies by teams of cult members who roam through airports,

shopping centers, offices, factories, and suburban neighborhoods, driven by a need to meet daily quotas that would dismay even the best of Fuller Brush men or Avon ladies.

To fill their quotas, the Moonies are taught how to "chant-
pray-run" while practicing "Heavenly Deception"—misleading customers into believing that their money is going to feed
starving children or combat drug abuse. When Christopher
Edwards, another former Moonie, objected to the practice of
Heavenly Deception, the head of his flower-selling team re-
torted:

> So what? It's for his soul and the glory of Heaven. Look,
> wouldn't you deceive a little to save the man's soul? . . . It's turn-
> ing Satan against himself, using Satan's money to build the Heav-
> enly Kingdom.

Chanting, praying, running through grueling eight-hour days
with time out only for eating a grapefruit, former Moonie Barbara Underwood confesses she wanted to make "millions of
dollars" to purchase and maintain hotels, resorts, palatial res-
idences from Chicago to New Orleans, training and living centers, college campuses, yachts, and even the Empire State and
Pan Am buildings. "Instilled in us was the firm belief that
Moon must reclaim all ownership of money and land from
Satan's stockpile." "Christians think that the Messiah must
be poor and miserable," says a Unification Church training
manual. "He did not come for this. Messiah must be the richest. Only He is qualified to have dominion over things. Otherwise, neither God nor Messiah can be happy."

The point is that humankind's religious impulses are more
often than not as much instrumentalities in the struggle for
worldly wealth, power, and physical well-being as manifesta-
tions of the search for spiritual salvation.

In romantically extolling the contemplative nature of Asian
spirituality, Western observers often overlook what ordinary
people as distinguished from a handful of saints and ascetic

holy men expect from Asian religion. I found that most Hindu believers were far more interested in praying for the rains to come, for their sick child to get well, and for their cow to have calves than in achieving transcendental bliss through meditation.

The point is that finding God and getting rich are not necessarily polar opposites. Both offer "final solutions" to overwhelming problems that seem insolvable by ordinary means. Anthropologists who have studied the South Seas "cargo cults" have long been aware that there is a meeting ground on which wealth and spirit commingle. Natives join cargo cults in order to induce their ancestors to return and make them wealthy. A similar note was struck by the Yurok of Northern California who were firmly convinced that they could become wealthy by persistently thinking about their cowrie shell money. They would go to the forest mumbling and wailing the refrain, "I want to be rich," until they began to have visions and saw cowrie shells hanging from the trees.

And that brings us to the modern-day California *I-want-to-be-rich* religion known as the Church of Hakeem. Members make donations which within seventy to ninety days are returned, "increased" up to four times the original amount. Chief minister Hakeem Abdul Rasheed, "master teacher" and "maker of millionaires," claims the increases come from God and that they are the fruits of "a reawakening of religious spirit." The police claim they come from a "Ponzi scheme" —a swindle named after a Boston con artist who paid early investors 50 percent interest out of the principal supplied by a rapidly broadening base of later investors. At celebrations held in cavernous old movie theaters, Hakeem exhorts his congregation to banish all doubts and negative thinking. Like the Yurok of old, as the crowd feels the spirit descending, they chant in unison: "Richer Faster, Richer Faster, Richer Faster." Hakeem calls out the names of ministers whose "increases" have arrived. They rush to the stage amid wild applause.

"I wanna hear you say 'Amen,' " Hakeem cries.

"Amen," the crowd roars.

Partisans of the Asiatic spirituality theory might argue that the Church of Hakeem is not an acceptable example of America's Third Great Awakening because it is too "worldly" to be a religion. Naturally, if one defines religion in such a way as to exclude "I-want-to-be-rich" themes, the Awakening will appear to be mainly concerned with spiritual rather than material problems. But there really is no sharp break between spiritual and material themes in contemporary American culture. Even the California-style pyramid clubs which spread across the United States toward the end of the 1970s bear more than a slight resemblance to a religious movement, and in a sense they are more representative of the spiritual ferment in America than communitarian sects such as the Hare Krishnas or the Divine Light Mission.

Like many other cults, pyramids get founded by charismatic directors who recruit the upper-level members of the pyramid. In a typical club, the founder prepares the pyramid chart and induces sixteen people to put up an entry fee. The first sixteen paying members must in turn recruit a total of thirty-two additional investors. Half of the entry fee goes to the person immediately above the recruit and half to the person at the top of the chart. When the chart is full, the pyramid splits and the people on various levels advance to the next highest level. With a one-thousand-dollar entrance fee, and a thirty-two-member base, the founder-director stands to win sixteen thousand dollars.

All players have an equal incentive to fill the chart. The person at the top wants the full sixteen thousand dollars while those at the bottom want to advance as quickly as possible to the next level where they will at least recoup their investment. This produces an instantaneous sense of fellowship among the participants. Clubs meet in private homes where refreshments are served and members pep each other up by singing their pyramid song and listening to testimonials from people who

152

have "topped out." Guests are urged to come forward and join up. Tearful jubilation reigns with each announcement that another slot on the chart has been filled and as the entrance fee—always in cash—is passed on from the newest member to those in the upper levels. At large meetings there can be a rush to fill the pyramid on a first-come first-serve basis and thousands of dollars in cash are exchanged among people who moments ago were perfect strangers, amid wild cheering and applause. Observers have not failed to note the cultlike religious overtones of the experience:

> The meetings themselves are reminiscent of a box social or an old-time revival. Previous winners are called up to testify, which they do with all the fervor of a bible-belt circuit rider. Like born-again supplicants, converts come forward to be anointed with a list, and drop $1000 in the collection plate.

For many Americans the single most shocking and puzzling event of the decade took place on November 18, 1978, in a jungle clearing in Guyana. "Hit men" from the Guyana branch of a California cult called The People's Temple ambushed and killed Congressman Leo Ryan and several of his aides, TV reporters, and would-be defectors. Shortly thereafter, the cult's leader, Jim Jones, and more than nine hundred followers ended their lives in what the news media first described as the largest "mass suicide" in modern history.

Can the theory that the new religious consciousness represents a turning away from the search for wealth and power explain the tragedy of Jonestown? I think not. It seemed to be otherwise at first because the world came to know The People's Temple as the "suicide cult." According to the headlines, the deceased had voluntarily poisoned themselves by drinking a mixture of cyanide, tranquilizers, and strawberry Flavor-Aid. It was as if the thirst for spiritual fulfillment had grown so obsessive that Jones's followers no longer placed the least value on their corporeal existence. But it is now known that Jonestown's "suicide" was the end product of a long frustrated quest for material as well as spiritual fulfillment; that members of the cult had become subject to Jones's maniacal will as much through chicanery, threats, and physical coercion as through devotion and faith, and that many who died during the final "white night" were murdered.

Jones, who claimed Native American ancestry, concentrated on recruiting blacks, especially older men and women who were on Social Security or who had small bank accounts or a little real estate. On joining, recruits signed their Social Security checks, bank accounts, and other property over to the Temple. In return, Jones promised to protect them from the coming nuclear holocaust and to cure them of cancer.

To increase the cult's cash flow, Jones hit upon the idea of having cult members adopt children who were wards of the State of California and therefore eligible for subsistence benefits under a variety of welfare programs.

At his Sunday services, Jones earned a reputation for curing cancer and raising the dead. In his cancer-cure act, Jones pointed at a man or woman in the audience and told them that although they didn't know it, they had cancer of the stomach. Aides rushed the terrified individual to the toilet and made them sit down. When the supposed cancer victims arose, the aides dredged a mass of rotten chicken livers from the bowl and brought it back for the audience to see. On other occasions, aides popped a bit of putrid liver down the throat of an hysterical subject who promptly gagged and vomited up the offending "cancer" in plain view of the congregation. To raise people from the dead, Jones had his aides knock themselves out with drugs and then conveniently "restored them to life" when the effects wore off.

Fearing that defectors would bring the Temple crashing down on his head, Jones surrounded himself with armed bodyguards and began to punish and humiliate anyone suspected of disloyal inclinations. Punishments included whipping, beating, forced nudity, and confessions of real or alleged homosexuality or adultery. When newspeople and public officials began to investigate the charge that at least one defector had been murdered, Jones decided to move the cult from San Francisco to Guyana.

The old people and the dependent children went first, secretly, in order to keep the welfare checks coming. When defectors and relatives back home found out what was happening they stepped up their efforts to have the cult investigated. Jones retaliated by threatening to have the whole settlement commit suicide. Day and night over the camp's public address system, Jones told his followers that they were about to be attacked and tortured to death by the CIA. Repeatedly he called them out of their beds, and, with armed guards standing by, forced them to drink harmless Flavor-Aid which he said was poisoned. With no means of escape from Jonestown (Jones held their passports and their money), wearied by the unaccustomed heat and humidity, constant physical labor in the fields, endless false alarms and threats of torture, many cult members, especially the older men and women, began to see suicide as a possible solution to their problems.

Congressman Ryan arrived in Jonestown with a congressional aide, representatives of the news media, including a crew from NBC's *Today* show, and a delegation of concerned relatives. Fifteen Temple members asked to leave with Ryan's party. Jones decided that he had no alternative but to order his hit men into action. From the tapes which Jones left behind and from the eyewitness accounts of a handful of survivors it is clear that some of the people of Jonestown did not take their own lives but were murdered. At least one-third of the residents were children under the age of sixteen. Few of their deaths can be considered completely "voluntary." Jones, resourceful to the end, ordered parents to administer the lethal poison to their children first. "I want my babies first. Take my babies and children first," he said as the camp's nurses set down the battered washtub full of cyanide. Children who

155

balked were held while Temple officials squirted the poison down their throats with syringes. With the children dying before their eyes, it was easier to get parents to drink the potion "voluntarily." Many adults accepted their fate more or less passively; others resisted, even under threat of being shot by the hit men who kept herding them forward toward the tub. Those who refused to take the poison had it forced down their throats. "As they spit it up, another syringe was squirted into their mouths until they finally gave up." It was easy to do this with the seniors, many of whom were feeble, sick, and senile. "Old men were held to the ground and juice was forced down their throats."

I wonder if the larger implications of the Jonestown tragedy have been misunderstood. By emphasizing the seemingly inexplicable and voluntary nature of the "mass suicide," the news media drew attention away from the palpable hardships and well-grounded fears which enabled Jones to recruit his followers in the first place and to keep them in line after they became dependent on him. Like tens of millions of other ordinary people, Jones's followers felt weak, neglected, isolated. They were under intense pressure from the rising costs of housing and medical care and the high incidence of street crimes. And as blacks, many of them had experienced the stings of racism and had grown weary of being treated as inferior citizens. Bizarre as their solution to these problems may seem, would it not be a mistake to ignore the similarity between them and the many millions of other Americans who also now feel defenseless and isolated and who, bewildered by the great changes that have swept across the land since World War II, have sought both spiritual solace and material well-being in the Third Great Awakening?

For whatever the balance may be between worldly and other-worldly themes in the cults that have adopted aspects of Asian religions, such cults are not representative of the main thrust of religious change in the United States today. It is not the rainbow of exotic movements that epitomizes the new religious consciousness. The entire spectrum of exotic, non-Western "psycho-mystico-parascientific-spiritual-therapeutic" phenomena actually constitutes only a small and atypical manifestation of America's religious and spiritual ferment. From the standpoint of impact on social and economic policy, numbers of believers and size of material base, the center of the Third Great Awakening, just like that of the previous Great Awakenings, lies squarely within the historic mainstream of American Protestantism. While at the most, three million ex-hippies, flower children, and drug dropouts of the 1960s were chanting, running, praying, "est-ing," "clearing," primal screaming, Rolfing, and so forth, at least ten times that number of Americans were finding religion by becoming "born-again" Christians.

Neither among the leaders of the born-again movement, nor among their followers, can I detect the influence of Asian-inspired religions. On the contrary, I think that the largest and fastest-growing center of the movement—which in fact lies at the heart of the entire Third Great Awakening—namely, the so-called video or television churches, bears a closer resemblance to a worldly Church of Hakeem or even to a California-style pyramid club than to Buddhism or Hinduism. As in the historic mainstream of American Protestantism, the born-again movement incorporates elements of a personal "gospel of wealth" in which material success and physical well-being are signs of God's grace to the individual true believer—to those who lead as well as to those who follow.

Evangelical Protestantism, unlike other religious cults, sects, and movements, has relied on television, America's most powerful medium of communication, to build its material base. While the Moonies were out scuffling for souls on street corners, and the Scientologists and encounter groups were registering handfuls of potential recruits for classes and seminars at expensive weekend retreats, a new generation of evangelists perfected the art of beaming themselves into the homes, apartments, trailers, and motel rooms of America's lost, frightened, and bewildered common man and woman. Yogis, Swamis, Sris, and Don Juans claim to be able to lie on beds of nails, levitate, and fly through the air; but the new breed of evangelists can do something far more impressive: They can bounce their images off Comstar I communication satellites and beam themselves down into every city and town in North America.

Not that the success of video Protestantism is only a matter of the medium. No, it is also very much a result of matching the content of the evangelical message to the needs of TV's religious consumers, many of whom are sick, old, or isolated, impoverished by inflation, bewildered by the changes in sex mores and the family, and frightened by crime in the streets. The television faithful form a community of suffering believers through the imagery on their screens. Unlike the members of communitarian cults, TV Christians need not uproot themselves from home, job, or family in order to participate in the healing and soothing powers of a caring and supportive fellowship. All they need do is send in twenty dollars and turn on the set. The evangelists and their aides talk directly to them. If they feel the need for two-way communication, a battery of volunteers is ready to receive their calls twenty-four hours a day.

With some justification, the new TV churches have been called "video cults." Critics argue that what separates them from the Hare Krishnas or the Moonies is merely their privileged position with respect to the mainstream of American Protestantism. But the word "cult" carries with it the connotation of being a small, arcane group, which is certainly not true of the TV churches with their millions of believers and their six-hundred-million-dollar annual gross income.

In conformity with the gospel of wealth, the most successful TV evangelists have a well-known penchant for luxurious homes, expensive cars, planes, and yachts. Evangelist Rex Humbard, for example, whose weekly Cathedral of Tomorrow services are broadcast over more than six hundred and fifty

North American TV stations, lives in a $650,000 family compound near Palm Beach, drives a Lincoln, and refuses to divulge his annual personal income, although it is known that his organization grosses twenty-five million a year. A Cleveland newspaper—*The Cleveland Press*—quoted Humbard as saying: "My people don't give a hoot what I spend that money for." Humbard's information officer denied this: "What he said was that 'people don't care what I spend my own money for.' " Either way, it is clear that Humbard's followers not only don't care what he spends on himself, but they would think there was something wrong if he didn't live better than the average American.

Video church members expect help in solving practical problems. The best way of proving one's ability to solve problems for others is to show that one can solve them for oneself. And so in the video church nothing succeeds like success. All of the leading figures in the electronic ministry have rags-to-riches stories to tell and their congregations hope to follow the same road at least part of the way.

Jim Bakker and his wife Tammy, whose PTL (Praise The Lord) club grossed over fifty million dollars in 1980, were an unknown penniless husband-wife gospel team before they started appearing on television. In his autobiography, Bakker cites fifty-five specific instances in which God responded to his pleas for money, cures, or other physical remedies. On two occasions he wrote checks for twenty thousand dollars knowing that his bank account was empty but that God would somehow provide the money before the checks bounced. Bakker not only expects God to make deposits for him but he also expects God to answer his prayers for parking places. Bakker and his wife take out about one hundred thousand dollars a year in salaries. But Bakker's brother, his parents, and his sister are all on the payroll as well. Among the "perks" that go with being the head of a television network with about two hundred broadcast affiliates (more than ABC has) was the gift of a $200,000 house by a wealthy contributor. PTL's mansion

159

headquarters in Charlotte, North Carolina, has a crystal chandelier, Oriental rugs over solid mahogany decor. Bakker's office is paneled in mahogany and has a black marble fireplace.

While not going quite so far as Sun Myung Moon's "Messiah must be the richest," the video evangelists are committed to the good life for themselves, and if possible, for their followers as well. According to Bakker, "The scripture says, 'Delight yourself in the Lord and he'll give you the desires of your heart' . . . Give and it shall be given unto you." In his book Bakker tells how one man prayed for a Winnebago mobile home, color brown, and got just that. Says Bakker: "Diamonds and gold aren't just for Satan—they're for Christians, too."

Pat Robertson, whose 700 Club grosses $58 million a year, finds no need to apologize for the twenty-million-dollar Persian-carpeted, marble-floored Virginia headquarters of his Christian Broadcasting Network. Ditto for California evangelist Robert Schuller and his Crystal Cathedral with its 10,250 one-way mirrors set in filigreed steel.

"I'm something of a show barker," Schuller cries out to the unchurched. "Come in here, there's something good inside for you." He wants the Crystal Church to be the "most talked-about religious building of the twentieth century because it is a testimony that his 'possibility thinking' works and that it can relieve the impatience, anxiety, and financial frustration from which our culture and its people suffer," writes David Singer in *Christianity Today*. If that does not suffice to silence critics who wonder why a born-again Christian could not find something better to do with sixteen million dollars, Schuller points to the church's 4,100 "income-producing seats" with which he intends to expand his ministerial services. Says Schuller: "Only a materialist, not a Christian, would be reluctant to invest money in people services."

On his Old Time Gospel Hour, Moral Majority Leader Jerry Falwell asks the faithful to turn over one-tenth of their income: "Christ has not captured a man's heart until He has your pocketbook." Two million potential contributors whose names and addresses are kept in a computer data bank receive frequent requests for money, one of which reads:

> Maybe your financial situation seems impossible. Put Jesus first in your stewardship and allow him to bless you financially.

Most video evangelists are also in the business of selling special-edition Bibles, autobiographies, and inspirational tracts. In addition, some of the video evangelists try to market the equivalent of what the Catholic Church used to call "relics"—holy objects blessed by their proximity to the saints and apostles. Finding himself fifty million dollars short of the funds needed to complete his City of Faith hospital complex near Tulsa, Oklahoma, video evangelist Oral Roberts baited one of his calls for help with swatches from a "miracle cloth." "My hands feel as if there is a supernatural heat in them," he declared. "My right hand is especially hot right now." Following God's instructions, Roberts began to turn out millions of swatches imprinted with his hot right hand. Those who acquire the cloth in return for purchasing a share in Miracle City at thirty-eight dollars a square foot, may expect to enjoy "special miracles."

But the video church has gone far beyond such traditional means of raising funds. The most widely viewed and most rapidly expanding programs use a television talk show format in combination with an ingenious variety of faith healing and Hakeem Abdul Rasheed "ministries of increase." As in the People's Temple, miraculous cures of illness, especially of cancer, play a central role in convincing the audience to join the congregation and to contribute money to spread the word and expand membership. But by exploiting the fact that there are millions of viewers in the electronic audience, the video evangelists can do away with the necessity of staging miracles or resorting to sleight of hand or other cheap tricks. Ingeniously, the intent is not to cure the people who are being watched, but to cure those who are watching and can't be seen. This removes any lingering temptation to outdo the likes of Jim Jones in conjuring up chicken liver tumors or in raising drugged assistants from the dead. Video miracles result from firing off a giant electronic shotgun. Down on his knees, hands raised to heaven, 700 Club evangelist Robertson prays: "O Lord, heal cancers right now! Thank you, Jesus. Thank you, Lord. Supply financial needs right now, in the name of Jesus! Thank you, Lord." As the "Word of Knowledge" descends, Robertson begins to see off-screen miracles happening "all over the nation":

> There is a woman in Kansas City who has a sinus. The Lord is drying that up right now. Thank you, Jesus. There is a man with a financial need—I think a hundred thousand dollars. That need is being met right now, and within three days the money will be supplied through the miraculous power of the Holy Spirit. Thank you, Jesus! There is a woman in Cincinnati with cancer of the lymph nodes. I don't know whether it's been diagnosed yet, but you haven't been feeling well, and the Lord is dissolving the cancer, right now! There is a lady in Saskatchewan in a wheel chair—curvature of the spine. The Lord is straightening that out right now and you can stand up and walk! Just claim it and it's yours. Stand up and walk. Thank you Jesus! Amen, and Amen!

Almost immediately the studio phones start lighting up with calls from people "claiming" some of the miracles. Among the three million viewers there is likely to be a woman in Kansas City who "has a sinus," a man *somewhere* in the United States or Canada who needs one hundred thousand dollars to save the family farm, a woman in Cincinnati who is convinced she has cancer of the lymph nodes, and a lady in a wheelchair in Saskatchewan, who just might manage to straighten up and walk to the phone.

Aides interview the "miracle claimers" and if they are personable and convincing, they are invited to appear on the show to bear witness to Robertson's gifts.

PTL Club Jim Bakker follows the same format:

> There is a prostate gland condition that God is healing right now. . . . There is a spinal condition, perhaps a missing disk, that is being restored. . . . Someone to my left has a kidney ailment . . . there are growths and in the name of Jesus those growths are gone. . . . You will not need surgery . . . there is something that goes into the marrow of the bone, maybe it's leukemia . . . the Lord is healing it.

Again the phones start lighting up. PTL and the 700 Club handle over a million and a quarter calls from viewers per year. Over twenty thousand viewers call in to each club to say that they have been healed. Others call in to tell how turning on the TV set led to saving their marriages, landing jobs, finding long-lost relatives, and other miracles. Many people simply call in to talk to the telephone counselors about their problems. The counselors take each caller's name and address and add them to the club's mailing list. From there on, they will begin to receive a steady stream of requests for contributions and announcements of special Bibles and other religious items which they can purchase.

If the reported miracles are not genuine, the onus rests with the people in the audience, not with the evangelists. Says Robertson: "We get about 25,000 reports a year from people who are healed. . . . All we can say is if they are all wrong, there are an awful lot of liars out there."

The true genius of Robertson and Bakker is that they were the first to see that by using TV they could operate Reverend Hakeem Abdul Rasheed's ministry of increase without being charged with running an illegal Ponzi scheme. Robertson calls his systems the "Kingdom Principles": The Bible says the more you give to Jesus the more you will get back in return. And the harder it is to give, the greater will be the increase. If you're poor and in debt, therefore, the best thing you could do for yourself would be to send the rent money to Robertson who will do Jesus' work with it. When Robertson finishes explaining how sending money to him might be profitable, his "straight man" dashes up with a report from one of the telephone counselors about a woman in California:

> She's on a limited income, and with all sorts of health problems, too. She decided to trust in God and to step out in faith on the Kingdom Principles. She was already giving half her disability money to the 700 Club to spread the gospel of Jesus Christ. But just last week, she decided to go all the way, and to give God the money she spends for cancer medicine—$120 a month. And three days later—get this!—from an entirely unexpected source, she got a check for three thousand dollars!

To which Robertson adds:

> Praise God! Let's give God a hand! And I wouldn't be surprised if God doesn't do something about that cancer, too. You there at home, if you want miracles, just step out in faith on the Kingdom Principle, and see what God is willing to do for you.

Like all great ideas, Bakker and Robertson's version of the ministry of increase is not completely original. Would it be too cynical of me to point out that in horse racing circles randomly aimed predictions are the business of people called "touts"? A man strikes up a conversation with you and tells you he's got a hot tip on horse number six in the seventh race. But he has already given hot tips to other bettors on horses one through five in the same race. Since there are only six horses running, one of the tips will pay off. If your horse wins, the tout will find you when you step up to the window to collect your money. "I have another hot tip for you in the next race," he says, "how about cutting me in on your take?" It seems like a harmless scheme unless you happen to be one of those people who bet their cancer medicine money on a hot tip that didn't win. And such people are always in the majority. Even if we credit Bakker and Robertson with fifty thousand genuine miracles a year among their five million viewers, that still leaves nine hundred and ninety people in every thousand out of luck.

It should be clear by now why I think it is incorrect to portray America's religious and spiritual ferment as a disembodied search for religious meaning. In the evangelical Protestant churches no less than in The People's Temple, worldly means to spiritual salvation tend to become ends in themselves. And however unpalatable it may seem, Ponzi schemes, pyramid clubs, and racetrack gambling are as much a part of America's Third Great Awakening as meditation, prayer, and faith.

At bottom, the Third Great Awakening is primarily a desperate response to the unsolved problems of malfunctioning consumerism, inflation, the upending of sex roles, breakup of the breadwinner family, alienation from work, oppressive government and corporate bureaucracies, feeling of isolation and loneliness, fear of crime, and bewilderment about the root cause of so many changes happening at once. Given all these unsolved problems, perhaps the question we should have been considering is not why the cults have spread but why they haven't spread more.

History confirms the fact that as expansionist cults and churches consolidate their material bases, they find it increasingly difficult to refrain from seeking solutions to worldly problems through political and economic power rather than through miracles. The role played by the conservative evangelicals in the 1980 elections can be interpreted as additional evidence of the increasingly worldly thrust of the Third Great Awakening.

No one knows where the road that elevates faith over reason will take America. But can it be too early to warn of the dangers that lie in theocracy? Can it be too soon to wonder if America's Third Great Awakening is the beginning of a "white night" in Jonestown played on a national scale?

9

Why America Changed

At the beginning of this book, we set out to see if America's cultural crisis was understandable as a response to the growth of bureaucracy and oligopoly, and to changes in the nature of work, and in the composition of the labor force. How useful has this idea been for explaining why there is so much that is new and strange in America today? Has it been able to show the interconnectedness of changes that seem to be unrelated? Let us go back to the beginning and sum up the main arguments.

The principal point of departure was that since the end of World War II, the United States has become a bureaucratized and oligopolized country, oriented more to people-processing and information-processing than to the production of goods. What was once a decentralized manufacturing society has become a centralized service and information-processing society. And equally important, what was once a society where women stayed home to work has become a society where women leave home to work.

Why did America's decentralized, individualistic, free-enterprise, goods-producing economy turn into a centralized, regulated, bureaucratized service-and-information-producing economy? Processes operating in both the private sector and in the government have to be considered. Let me review those in the private sector first. Through mergers and acquisitions, a handful of giant companies gained ascendancy in manufacturing, trade, commerce, transport, farming, mining, and energy production. In a sense this had to happen. It was a development inherent in the practice of free enterprise. Some corporations were bound to succeed more than others; some were bound to swallow, and others to be swallowed by their competitors. Some would go out of business; others would grow to giant size. To say that this process was "inherent" is not to say that it was inevitable. The United States instituted anti-monopoly laws, but it failed to institute anti-oligopoly laws. Yet the consequences of oligopoly are very similar to the consequences of monopoly. For example, take prices. With only a handful of giant corporations dominating a given industry, prices tend to be set by the costs of production rather than demand and supply in the marketplace. This allows for the growth of layers of redundant and inefficient administrators, office workers, promotional specialists, and sales help. It also encourages the toleration of inefficiencies and redundancies in union contracts which impede the substitution of machines for labor and which force up wage rates faster than productivity.

Turning to the government sector, one can readily understand why oligopoly and bureaucracy were fostered by the continuous enlargement of government agencies at the federal, state, and local levels. Again, one can argue that this development was a highly predictable (but not inevitable) consequence of having a capitalist economy with its cycle of booms and busts. After 1932 there was little choice but to seek to modify the effects of the business cycle by manipulating taxes, interest rates, money supply, enlarging the civil service, subsidizing jobs, and by doling out various kinds of welfare payments and subsidies to individuals and corporations. That is why the U.S. government set off on the road to becoming the largest employer in the United States and the second largest multinational conglomerate in the world (second only to the Soviet Union).

The reason for the turn from goods production to service-and-information production is far less obvious than the reason for the growth of corporate oligopoly and big government. It was a matter of needs and opportunities. In the name of efficiency, goods production became automated, concentrated, unionized. Hence the labor market could no longer grow by adding goods-producing jobs.

Yet something had to be done to accommodate the increasing numbers of people who were looking for work. Not that the whole expansion of service-and-information jobs was planned as a national make-work scheme. But the closing down of job opportunities in goods-production meant that an enormous labor force was becoming available for white- and pink-collar enterprises which had not yet been automated or unionized. The relative cheapness of the nonunionized white- and pink-collar workers encouraged private businesses to expand their investment in information-processing and the production of services. At the same time, wasn't the increase in government employees a less provocative expedient for coping with the unemployment problem than putting twenty million extra people on the dole?

Now we are on the way toward understanding the epidemic of shoddy goods, catastrophic disservices, and shrinking dollars. After three decades of the most astonishing labor-saving technological advances in the history of the human species, everything became more expensive. Why? Because at the same time that factory automation was saving labor and raising productivity, something else was wasting labor and lowering productivity on an even grander scale. It seems to me that this something else was none other than the rise of public and private bureaucratic oligopolies and the shift from a predominantly blue-collar to a predominantly pink- and white-collar labor force. People who work in and for bureaucracies whether at white-collar, pink-collar, or blue-collar jobs, become inflexible, bored, and alienated. They may turn out more products, information, or services per unit-time but the quality of what they produce suffers. And so let us face up to an unpleasant truth: By lowering quality, industrial bureaucracy can waste labor as fast as industrial machinery can save it.

Bureaucracy and oligopoly can be even more costly when it comes to producing services and information rather than goods. Bureaucracies and oligopolies (government or private) do not stop at wasting labor; they actively produce disservices and misinformation which may range from inconveniences to life-shattering ordeals for customers or clients. From a holistic perspective, therefore, the main cause of inflation has been the deteriorating quality of goods and services produced by inefficient bureaucracies and oligopolies. Several intermediary causes help to round out this picture. For example, economists emphasize the ever-increasing burden of debt being shouldered by government, businesses, and consumers. Debt is inflationary since borrowing money from a bank is equivalent to putting more money in circulation (the banks back only a small proportion of what they lend with liquid assets). The more dollars in circulation, the less each dollar can buy unless there is an equivalent increase in the value of marketable goods and services. It is true that in quantity the amount of goods and services did increase, but this was canceled out by the qualitative decline of these same goods and services. Hence the real value of goods and services did not increase as fast as the money supply.

What prompted the rise in debt? I suggest that it was none other than the decreasing efficiency of this oligopolized and bureaucratized economy. Government went into debt to finance its huge bureaucratic expansion, because real taxable income was not growing as fast as government expenditures. Private corporations went into debt for a similar reason: They were not efficient enough to expand their production out of the income generated from sales.

To make matters worse, as the dollar shrank, long-term loans became hard to find. Interest rates rose, creating acute cash-flow problems which the corporations met by quality-destroying expedients such as planned obsolescence and the debauchery of brand names.

Many economists have also pointed to the inflationary effects of the price-administering powers of the corporate oligopolies. The weakening of price competition buffered the oligopolies from the normal free-market effects of business depressions and rising unemployment rates. By their ability to set prices to cover costs regardless of falling demand, the oligopolies helped to create the unprecedented problem known as stagflation. But government had a hand in this also. After all, whether for humanitarian or selfish political reasons, it was the government that refused to let the Great Depression return during which inefficient oligopolies would either have had to lower prices or go out of business.

The depletion of natural resources, especially of fossil fuels, has also had an inflationary impact. Yet productivity gains associated with automation and other technological advances were more than sufficient to cancel out the rising cost of fuel had these technological advances themselves not been canceled out or held back by bureaucratic bungling, inefficiency, and waste. One might even say that had it not been for the oligopoly structure of the petroleum corporations, alternative and cheaper sources of energy would have been developed long before the depletion of domestic oil reserves reached crisis proportions.

Now we have some idea why inflation and shoddy goods and catastrophic disservices went hand in hand with the switch to a predominantly service-and-information-oriented economy. The next step is to show that these same developments provided the conditions responsible for wrenching women out of the home and into the job market. I think it happened this way:

Married women needed to find jobs because the male bread-winner's take-home pay did not increase fast enough after 1960 to feed, clothe, house, transport, and educate the children of the baby boom. Although officially the inflation rate was insignificant until after 1965, the era of planned obsolescence and catastrophic disservices had already begun well before then.

But one must explain not only why women wanted jobs but why the jobs wanted women. The jobs wanted women because they were low-paying nonunionized people-processing and word-processing jobs. Not only did women have the literacy and other educational credentials for office jobs, retail sales, teaching, nursing, and other white- and pink-collar services, but they were initially willing to accept part-time and temporary work and less pay than breadwinner males with comparable credentials.

While this shift was taking place, no one realized that it would act as an interface between great changes occurring in the political and economic spheres and equally great changes that were about to occur in the family and sexual spheres. As prices zoomed and quality problems became more severe, women found themselves locked into the wage labor force. The entire marital and procreative complex surrounding housewifery and motherhood came into conflict with the physical and psychological demands placed upon women in their child-rearing and wage-earning roles. In conformity with the "feminine mystique" women were supposed to accept a subordinate position both in the home and at their jobs. This made some sense as long as the breadwinner male brought home the bread; but as the cost of rearing children zoomed upwards, the wife-mother's second income became essential for couples with middle-class aspirations. The sentimental veneer—the "mystique"—covering up the exploitation inherent in the traditional sex roles began to peel off. The entire edifice of the marital and procreative imperative with its Victorian double standards and its patriarchal prudery began to crumble. Down came the fertility and first-time marriage rates. Up went the

171

divorce rate, consensual liaisons, delayed marriages, childless and one-child families, and a whole new antiprocreationist and libertine sexual consciousness.

With a substantial majority of younger men and women committed to the proposition that sex is primarily for pleasure rather than for procreation, tolerance of and experiment with pornography, nonheterosexual, and nongenital relationships were bound to increase. It is no mystery therefore why homosexuals with their effective nonprocreative sex-for-joy relationships were emboldened to come out of the closet.

Of course powerful defenders of the old marital and procreative standards still remain. But even as the anti-abortion and anti-homosexual forces struggle with their adversaries, their own life-styles reflect the underlying shift toward more libertine sexual standards. The video evangelists (unlike the old-style fundamentalists), for example, are strongly committed to the proposition that sex-for-joy is a sacrament and that it is the Christian wife's duty to be attractive by wearing makeup and sexy lingerie. Noteworthy also is the isolation of the issue of abortion from that of contraception. With the fertility rate among Catholic right-to-life enthusiasts indistinguishable from that of pro-abortionists, it is difficult to interpret the right-to-life movement in the United States as being essentially pro-natal. Anti-abortion legislation would only inhibit the abortion rate among the poor, largely black women on welfare; one might conclude therefore that the real target of the right-to-life movement is the right of inner-city blacks to enjoy sex at government expense.

There are other aspects of America's cultural crisis for which the shift in women's status has played a crucial role. Some of these, specifically race relations, crime, and the decay of the inner cities, appear at first to be unrelated. Yet to ignore the connections is to bury one's head in the sand. Women are of course not responsible for the fact that information- and people-processing jobs increased while goods-producing jobs decreased. Nor were they responsible for the inflation that drove them into the job market. But one cannot ignore the devastating significance of this change for the inner-city black community. Black males have not been able to find work either in the shrinking job markets in agriculture, mining, and manufacture, nor in the people-processing and information-processing fields, where better-educated literate white women have had a strong competitive advantage over them. Bad as the plight of white employed females may be, the plight of the unemployed black male is worse.

Up to now the main burden of structural unemployment caused by automation has fallen upon inner-city men. Whites have shown little comprehension of why this has been the case and even less sympathy. Rather than pay the bill for a genuine system of relief and welfare, the white majority has sanctioned the growth of an insane system which rewards mothers of "fatherless" children with bonuses, while the fathers of such children are given neither welfare nor jobs and turn to crime as an alternative career. To repeat, my point here is not that white women are the cause of the structural unemployment of black males, but that the rhetoric of women's liberation has done much to obscure the interconnectedness of America's problems and the futility of trying to solve them separately by pressing for the short-run benefits of one special interest group, no matter how just its cause.

Finally, what is the explanation for the surge of interest in shamanism, exorcism, witchcraft, extraterrestrial beings, and expansionist cults and churches? There cannot be much doubt that the new religious consciousness reflects the bewilderment and insecurity engendered by rapid cultural change. But how shall we interpret the specific content of this "Awakening"? Does it signal the end of America's quest for earthly dominion, a retreat from consumerism and materialism, and the triumph of spiritual over practical needs? Or are we witnessing a desperate end-of-the-line attempt to achieve earthly dominion and material well-being by magical and supernatural means? The second hypothesis seems to me to be much closer to the truth.

If one studies the actual worldly involvements of the human-potential movement, the video-evangelist movement, and even that of the communitarian cults, there is very little evidence of an unalloyed commitment to spiritual transcendence. Why is this distinction important? Because in the first instance one sees a benign spiritualized America escaping from its material problems into mystical union with God; while in the second instance, one sees a dangerously frustrated America becoming increasingly receptive to charismatic, messianic, and fanatical solutions to its material problems.

America is in deep trouble; but let no one suppose that our plight cannot get a whole lot worse. Our standard of living—even with due consideration of its quality problems—is still among the highest on earth. And compared with most of the state-level societies that have ever existed, the degree of personal security and freedom enjoyed by the average U.S. citizen—except for the inner cities—is extraordinary. Can we find a way to defend, improve, and broaden the base of material welfare without giving up the cherished personal liberties which are America's splendid heritage?

The reader was warned not to expect a detailed set of prescriptions for restoring the American dream. In writing this book, I have proceeded on the premise that people cannot rationally offer a solution to a problem unless they understand its cause. It seems to me that if we act on the basis of sterile political formula, irrational impulses, or unsound knowledge, we are likely to make matters worse rather than better. The question of what or who is to blame for things falling apart, for catastrophic disservices, for stagflation, crime, and the rest haunts Americans of all political persuasions. Yet up to now there has been little public discussion of the root causes of these problems. Sad to say, by using technical jargon, and by pursuing isolated studies of interest only to specialists, the social sciences have been a source of confusion rather than of enlightenment as far as the vast majority of people is concerned.

Although I insist that it is important to achieve an objective and holistic understanding of U.S. social life prior to and independent of political action, the reader has a right to know what policy implications I draw from this work. One clear implication is that Americans are unlikely to acquiesce to cuts in their standard of living in the name of spiritual salvation. While it would be convenient to both Republicans and Democrats if America really were on the verge of renouncing the quest for material progress in favor of a life of "voluntary simplicity," or of born-again other-worldly austerity, I have found no evidence to support such a view. Hence, there is little prospect that administrations which fail to reverse the downward trend in living standards will survive the wrath of the electorate.

The current interest in abandoning the quest for universal material affluence reminds me of the pessimism which attended the birth of the industrial era. So strong was this view that at the beginning of the nineteenth century, economics came to be known as the "dismal science." Economists of the period held that there was no way to solve the problem of poverty. Drawing their inspiration from the work of Thomas Malthus, they gloomily predicted that if wages went up, population would increase, more people would enter the job market and wages would fall back down to poverty levels. Today a new breed of dismal scientists has come into existence. These new prophets of gloom no longer say that poverty is inevitable. But they insist that the American dream of universal prosperity will never come true. We must not permit ourselves to surrender to this vision of the future without a struggle.

The new dismal science was born toward the end of the 1960s amid dire warnings by ecologists about "limits to growth," global heat death from the burning of fossil fuels, and exhaustion of nonrenewable resources. These warnings have inspired a far-ranging philosophical and theological critique of the whole idea of material progress. According to social critic Jeremy Rifkin for example, there is no scientific basis for the belief in progress since the law of evolution is negated by the law of entropy. The entropy law states that energy flows from higher to lower levels and thereby guarantees the ultimate running down of the universe. Rifkin maintains that recognition of entropy as the supreme physical law demands that Americans abandon their dream of material affluence based on dominion over nature and dedicate themselves instead to conserving nature and getting rid of their possessions. Does your car give you trouble? The entropy ethic offers a simple solution: "If you don't own an automobile, you don't need to worry about steel-belted radials, gas lines, traffic tie-ups, and car thieves," writes Rifkin.

I would find the new dismal science more acceptable if it could be shown that the changes in U.S. culture discussed in previous chapters have been caused by ecological limits to growth. But where is the evidence that depletions account for a significant part of inflation, unemployment, terror in the streets, and the outpouring of shoddy goods and catastrophic disservices in America today? All of these problems had already reached excruciating levels by 1970 at the very height of the era of the cheapest energy supply the world had ever known. Moreover, the depletion of U.S. domestic oil reserves was not a natural disaster. It was a people-made disaster, foreseen and predicted (if not premeditated) and entirely evitable had alternate sources of energy been developed during the period when the United States was foolishly becoming dependent on importing oil from one of the most remote and politically unstable regions on earth.

The central fallacy of the new dismal science is that it interprets the present crisis in the light of a future crisis. Perhaps depletions of natural resources will indeed drag us down into an entropic death. But why impose a distant morbid possibility on a present that is still pregnant with life and hope? George Gilder, a staunch believer in the ability of unfettered capitalism to solve America's problems, suggests that the current infatuation with the idea of entropy as a substitute for the idea of progress may be more symptomatic of psychological rather than ecological stress:

> At a time when radically important new technologies are being spawned on every hand, leading experts imagine that we are entering a technological climacteric, a period of diminishing scientific returns. Such views are suitable for analysis not in the universities (where they often prevail) but on the couch.

While I find myself in substantial agreement with Gilder's arguments against no-growth pessimists, I cannot accept his standard right-wing Republican belief that America's problems will be solved simply by giving U.S. corporations a free hand to do business as they please. Is it realistic to expect that the deregulation of the private sector will cure the ills of hyper-industrialization? Left to their own devices, what will prevent the conglomerates from becoming even more oligopolized and bureaucratized than they already are? What will prevent them from producing more shoddy goods and catastrophic disservices, more chronic unemployment and poverty, and more broken families and terror in the streets?

Believers in unfettered capitalism profess to be concerned about improving the well-being of the poor, but it quickly becomes apparent that they are far more concerned about protecting the well-being of the rich. While the new dismal scientists want to solve the problem of poverty by abolishing everyone's material desires, the unfettered capitalists want to solve it by convincing the poor that they have only themselves to blame for not being rich. In his book, *Wealth and Poverty,* which has acquired something of the status of a holy scripture in unfettered capitalist circles, Gilder writes: "The first principle is that in order to move up, the poor must not only work, they must work harder than the classes above them." Hard-nosed capitalist-roader and woolly-brained entropy freak meet each other on common ground here, each proposing to change society by offering people less rather than more for helping to

177

solve America's cultural crisis. What Gilder fails to acknowledge is that people who can't find jobs can scarcely be expected to work harder than the "classes above them"—unless
he intends to exhort such people to work harder at muggings
and other disagreeable alternatives to welfare.

The ethic of unfettered capitalism, in other words, is no
more likely to provide a satisfactory solution to the current
crisis than the ethic of entropy. In the light of the contribution
of private oligopoly and bureaucracy to America's malaise,
what sense does it make to attack only government oligopoly
and bureaucracy? To restore quality in goods and services we
must reverse the trend toward economic concentration and
the mindless division of labor in both public and private
spheres of endeavor. If we act to remove all restraints on the
conglomerates, they will simply expand their production of
shoddy goods and catastrophic disservices, and continue to
inflate prices to cover up their inefficiencies. Furthermore,
there is not even a remote chance that by granting the conglomerates a freer hand they will create enough jobs in the
private sector to break the cycle of unemployment-crime-wel-
fare in the inner cities. In fact, there is a very high probability
that the demand for labor in the private sector will not be
sufficient to avoid a steady increase in "normal" unemployment. The immense effort now being launched to complete the
automation of goods-production by robotizing assembly lines,
in conjunction with the equally great effort to substitute micro-
chip computers for clerks, typists, receptionists, and sales
help, virtually guarantees that there will be more unemployment in the future.

It is true that similar dire predictions about the effect of
labor-saving devices were made during the 1950s and yet the
economy managed to find employment for thirty-five million
new workers. But as we now realize, almost all of these new
jobs were in the information-processing and people-processing
fields which temporarily escaped the main thrust of technological progress. Looking back over the past two hundred years
we can see that the sequence of industrial development has

moved inexorably from agriculture to manufacture and mining; and from manufacturing and mining to people- and information-processing. As productivity rose in agriculture, agricultural employment fell and the surplus labor was drawn off into manufacturing and mining; then as productivity in manufacturing and mining rose, surplus labor was drawn off into the production of information and services. What next?

With micro-chip computerization of information-and-service jobs the fastest growth industry in the United States, who can doubt that the same process is about to be repeated in the service-and-information fields? But with one difference: There is no conceivable realm of profitable employment whose expansion can make up for even modest productivity gains among the nation's sixty million service-and-information workers.

Before long, therefore, America will have to resolve the contradiction between saving labor and making jobs—between making people more productive and putting them out of work. Because of this structural contradiction, a policy of slashing taxes, shrinking the government bureaucracy, reducing welfare and deregulating the private sector cannot long endure. Pursuit of this policy may prevent a runaway inflation but it will add millions of middle-class white-collar workers— especially women—to the ranks of the jobless, and thereby further erode the standards of consumption of a substantial portion of the American people.

Since the major parties are well aware of the danger of runaway inflation on the one hand and of Great Depression unemployment on the other, both will want to follow middle-of-the-road strategies. Neither will admit that it has no plan for restoring the American dream of prosperity with freedom and justice for all. While muddling through from one election to another, each will concentrate on placating the demands of the most strident special-interest groups and single-issue constituencies in the hope that the rest of the people will not notice that the country is sinking into a pit of unknown depth.

How long will this period of creeping stagflation and covert subversion of the American dream last? The answer may depend on how long the burden of austerity can continue to fall on the inner cities and on how much force the white middle class is willing to see used against inner-city riots and crime. A lot depends also on the course of the arms race and on the ability of the incumbent parties to postpone their day of reckoning with the electorate by making austerity for the many, and socialism for the rich, a matter of patriotic duty.

Since the politics of muddling, temporizing, and prevaricating will not prevent a further rise in structural unemployment nor put an end to inflation, movements responsive to concrete and immediate solutions are bound to gain strength. Wage and price controls, federal subsidies to endangered corporations, and massive make-work programs may prove to be irresistible with the next swing of the political pendulum. One has merely to project world-wide trends toward centralized, bureaucratized industrial states to realize that other solutions are far less probable.

But what would this American super-state look like? In the "best case" scenario, America's great democratic heritage would prevail and civil liberties would not necessarily be destroyed. Perhaps the burden of austerity would be distributed more evenly, and the public transport system and the inner cities would be rebuilt by giant federal work and welfare programs, and perhaps violent street crimes would diminish. But is there not already sufficient evidence from the Soviet bloc and the Western welfare states that the penalties of bureaucracy and oligopoly would grow worse? If an America that is only half bureaucratized and oligopolized is already a cornucopia of shoddy goods, catastrophic disservices, and soul-deadening alienation, what reasons do we have to believe that this situation will improve when the country is totally bureaucratized and oligopolized? None that I know of.

Moreover the assumption that democratic institutions and civil liberties will flourish under a super government may not hold up. If the movement to create a totally bureaucratized and oligopolized economy takes place in an atmosphere of urban rioting, heightened international tensions, and military buildup, a grimmer scenario may unfold. As in George Orwell's morbid vision of 1984, there is a significant chance that the endangered political species known as Western democracy will become extinct, victim of a totalitarian takeover (from the right or the left—they would by then be hard to tell apart).

And finally, to move to the worst case, can we discount the possibility of a suicidal "white night" nuclear crusade led by born-again Christian ayatollahs hellbent on reasserting U.S. global military and economic hegemony? The nuclear stalemate rests entirely on the assumption that neither side wants to see the world annihilated. While the majority of born-again Christians certainly accepts this covenant with the future, can we ignore the fact that the idea of a military-messianic apocalypse lies at the very base of the Judeo-Christian tradition?

Must we then give up the American dream? Is there no way to avoid the known penalties of bureaucracy and oligopoly? Yes, there is a way. And that is to reverse the centralizing trend of industrialization. Resolution of America's cultural crisis could conceivably take the form of encouraging the development of small-scale private enterprises, manned by hard-driving, efficient, profit-sharing work teams producing enough of a surplus to pay for first-class educational and community services as well as for the compassionate care of the sick and the elderly. But is this a realistic proposal in view of the fact that no industrial society has yet managed to reverse the centralizing trend? My own personal feeling on this matter is that knowledge of the unwanted and detested features of the centralizing scenarios rationally compels us to consider the alternative of radical decentralization.

First of all, it is self-defeating to regard America's future as predetermined by the experiences of other nations. The heritage of private initiative, pragmatic knowhow, mechanical ingenuity, and grass roots town-hall democracy probably still runs stronger and deeper in the United States than anywhere else.

Moreover, while decentralization goes against the grain of

modern history, it need not go against the grain of human nature. Until recently, decentralization presented itself as a form of voluntary austerity, conjuring up images of iron pumps in muddy farmyards, and rooms lit by candlelight. But the technology of solar and other decentralized forms of energy production is rapidly advancing toward the point where small communities may be able to achieve relatively high per capita cash incomes from a variety of profit-making enterprises, in addition to enjoying the amenities of clean air and water, personal safety, and humane interpersonal relationships. The hope is that the decentralized configuration would spread not as a cult of poverty, nor as an otherworldly gospel of wealth, but as a down-to-earth practical means of achieving higher-quality goods and services and rising instead of falling consumption standards through elimination of bureaucracy and oligopoly and the unfettering of individual initiative.

All this will take time. I see no way of creating a decentralized society by means of a revolution aimed at dismembering America's public and private oligopolies. The existing organizations are too entrenched and powerful to be broken up all at once. Rather, decentralization will come about, if at all, as a result of a series of strategic decisions which can slowly tip the balance against the thralldom of hyper-industrialization. For example, very little progress can be made toward decentralization without scaling down America's military-industrial complex, and very little progress can be made in that direction unless some way can be found to lower international tensions and halt the arms race. Much also depends on stimulating the development of the right kind of solar and other forms of decentralized energy production, and of appropriate energy-efficient machinery to be used in small manufacturing plants and in the home. Equally important will be the development of legal barriers against takeovers of new energy technologies and decentralized industries by multinational conglomerates, and the passage of legislation favorable to small businesses and community-based cooperatives. Thus the creation of an affluent egalitarian, decentralized society may be a long way off, but decisions that open and shut doors for radically different kinds of futures will have to be made in the months and years immediately ahead.

Given the enormous power and formidable inertia of the hyper-industrial oligopolies and bureaucracies, there is only a slim chance of achieving a future more in accord with the vision of freedom and affluence on which past generations of Americans were nourished. Nonetheless, this chance is sufficient to support a rational hope of reversing the trends that have led to America's present malaise. The will to resist and to try for something better is an important component in the struggle against oligopoly and bureaucracy. Of course, to desire something strongly enough to fight for it does not guarantee success. But it changes the odds. The renewal of the American dream may be improbable, but it will become finally impossible only when the last dreamer gives up trying to make it come true.

References

The entries which follow supply references for specific viewpoints, facts, and all extended quotes. They appear in order of occurrence, chapter by chapter and page by page, and provide authors' names, date of publication, and page numbers. For full titles and complete names of authors and other standard reference information, consult the Bibliography.

Chapter 1. Introduction

page 13, line 26
Feyerabend, 1970
page 13, line 35
Silverman, 1975:75
page 14, line 9
Diamond, 1972:413
page 14, line 22
Dabney, 1980:50
page 15, line 2
Ibid.

Chapter 2. Why Nothing Works

page 17, line 20
Wall Street Journal, Dec. 16, 1980
page 18, line 11
New York Daily News, May 2, 1980
page 18, line 34
Quality Progress, April 1979:11
page 18, line 36
U.S. News & World Report, Sept. 6, 1976
page 19, line 6
Andreasen and Bert, 1977:94
page 19, line 11
New York Times, Sept. 19, 1979
page 19, line 36
Wall Street Journal Index, 1979:724–25
page 21, line 12
Wall Street Journal, Jan. 6, 1981
page 25, line 32
Galbraith, 1978:2
page 26, line 5
New York Times, Sept. 28, 1980
page 26, line 14
Business Week, June 30, 1980

page 27, line 16
Barnet and Müller, 1974:323ff.
page 27, line 16
Papanek and Hennessy, 1977:53
page 28, line 8
Juran, 1978:11
page 28, line 14
Op. cit., 16
page 28, line 37
Juran, 1974
page 30, line 13
Benstock, 1980:29
page 30, line 23
Wall Street Journal, Jan. 5, 1981
page 31, line 32
Wright, 1979:217–18
page 32, line 30
Business Week, June 30, 1980:78
page 33, line 4
Op. cit., 81
page 33, line 24
Barnet and Müller, 1974:354
page 34, line 25
Op. cit., 349–50
page 34, line 34
Vogel, 1979
page 35, line 2
Cohen, 1972:55
page 36, line 33
Juran, 1978:14
page 37, line 31
Carter and Dilatush, 1976:79

Chapter 3. Why the Help Won't Help You

page 39, line 12
New York *Times,* July 14, 1980
page 40, line 2
U.S. News & World Report, July 9, 1978
page 40, line 7
Personal anecdote
page 40, line 13
Anthony Lewis's column, New York *Times,* May 28, 1979

page 40, lines 23, 30
Personal anecdotes
page 40, line 36
Thanks to Martha Fried
page 41, line 24
Bell, 1973:130–31
page 41, line 26
Porat, 1980
page 42, line 35
Thanks to Augustus Lembo and Annette Zaner
page 45, line 2
Stanback, 1979:45
page 45, line 14
Job, 1980:40ff.
page 46, line 7
Howe, 1977:17
page 46, line 20
Bell, 1973:133
page 47, line 23
Braverman, 1974:314
page 47, line 31
Job, 1980:41
page 49, line 7
Braverman, 1974:4
page 50, line 15
Lasko, 1980:134ff.
page 50, line 20
New York *Times,* Sept. 19, 1979
page 51, line 18
Nussbaum, 1980:3
page 51, line 31
Ibid.
page 52, lines 17, 31
Op. cit., 9–12, 21
page 53, line 30
Braverman, 1974:340
page 54, line 5
Toffler, 1980:189
page 55, line 13
Consumer Affairs Division, N.J.
page 56, line 32
Sterling, 1979
page 57, line 21
Op. cit., 288

page 57, line 25
Singer, 1979:161

Chapter 4. Why the Dollar Shrank

page 60, line 20
Heilbroner and Thurow, 1981:3
page 61, line 24
Lekachman, 1980:16–17
page 62, line 2
Gordon, 1974:48ff.
page 63, line 25
U.S. Statistical Abstract, 1980:283
page 63, line 29
Thurow, 1980
page 64, line 24
Okun, 1980:3
page 65, line 13
Ringer, 1979:128; Porat, 1976:228
page 66, line 20
Bacon and Eltis, 1978
page 67, line 1
Wall Street Journal, Oct. 28, 1980
page 68, line 4
Thurow, 1980:7
page 68, line 8
Ibid.
page 68, line 26
Bacon and Eltis, 1978:214
page 69, line 23
Melman, 1974
page 72, line 6
Harrington, 1980:60
page 72, line 11
Ibid.
page 72, line 27
Magdoff and Sweezy, 1977:102
page 72, line 29
Barnet and Müller, 1974:271
page 74, line 15
Harrington, 1980:132
page 75, line 3
Lipsky, 1980:172

Chapter 5. Why Women Left Home

page 76, line 14
New York *Times,* September 1969
page 77, line 23
Deggler, 1980:436
page 77, line 32
Evans, 1979:211–13
page 79, line 1
Cudlipp, 1971:15
page 79, line 27
Montagu, quoted in Degler, 1980:440
page 79, line 30
Op. cit., 422
page 79, line 35
Hacker, 1961
page 80, line 35
U.S. Bureau of the Census, 1974:49
page 82, line 24
Seward, 1979
page 84, line 14
UNESCO, 1973:69
page 84, line 31
Smith-Rosenberg, 1978:238
page 85, line 17
Ploscowe, 1951
page 85, line 17
Drummond, 1953
page 86, line 14
Minge-Kalman, 1978
page 87, line 13
Degler, 1980:396
page 87, line 24
Epstein, 1970
page 87, line 35
Brownlee, 1979
page 88, line 2
Raphael, 1979
page 88, line 9
Westoff, 1978
page 88, line 21
Kolko, 1979
page 88, line 22
Smith, 1979
page 88, line 36
Ryscavage, 1979

page 89, line 25
Butz and Ward, 1979
page 89, line 25
Blake and Gupta, 1975
page 90, line 8
Margolis, 1977:28
page 90, line 15
Joint Economic Committee, 1980
page 91, line 6
Slater, 1979:20
page 91, line 6
Degler, 1980:419
page 91, line 12
Margolis, 1977:26
page 94, line 30
Pifer, 1978:4
page 94, line 35
Minge, 1981
page 94, line 35
Espenshade, 1977
page 94, line 35
Turchi, 1975
page 95, line 6
Wall Street Journal, Feb. 2, 1976
page 96, line 12
Bernard, 1980
page 96, line 20
Monthly Labor Review, April
1979:52
page 96, line 20
Degler, 1980:454
page 96, line 31
Harrington, 1980:85
page 97, line 5
*National Bureau of Economic
Research Reporter,* Fall 1979:2
page 97, line 8
Wattenberg and Reinhardt 1979:460

page 102, line 3
Adam, 1979:1
page 102, line 8
Wittman, 1977:330
page 102, line 12
Altman, 1973:186
page 103, line 29
Ford and Beach, 1970:263
page 104, line 3
Dover, 1978:103
page 104, line 7
Ungaretti, 1978
page 104, line 25
Bentham, 1978:392
page 106, line 2
Evans-Pritchard, 1970:1430, 1429
page 106, line 12
Kelly, 1976
page 108, line 11
Werner, 1979
page 110, line 19
Smith-Rosenberg, 1978:235
page 110, line 22
Bullough, 1976:121
page 112, line 2
Levine, 1979
page 113, line 15
Elshtain, 1979:498
page 113, line 31
Wolf, 1979:145–48
page 114, line 9
Hite, 1978:78
page 114, line 21
New York *Times,* May 9, 1979
page 114, line 27
Rollins, 1972
page 115, line 29
Friedan, 1979:92–94

Chapter 6. Why the Gays Came Out of the Closet

page 100, line 5
Wittman, 1977:344
page 101, line 15
Lee, 1979:179–80

Chapter 7. Why There's Terror in the Streets

page 116, line 25
U.S. National Criminal Justice
Information and Statistical
Service, 1978

pages 117–18
Griffith, 1978
page 118, line 34
Ross and Benson, 1979:77–78
page 119, line 11
Skogan, 1979:377
page 120, line 29
New York *Times*, April 12, 1981
page 121, line 6
Doleschal and Newton, 1979
page 122, line 22
U.S. National Criminal Justice
Information and Statistics Service,
1976:11
page 122, line 35
Hindelang, 1978:100
page 123, line 11
Mulvihill, Tumin, and Curtis, 1969
page 123, line 30
Hindelang, 1978:100
page 124, line 5
Ross and Benson, 1979:78
page 124, line 34
New York *Times*, Sept. 28, 1980
page 125, line 9
Brown, 1978:88–89
page 125, line 10
Conyers, 1978:678
page 126, line 7
Conyers, 1979:140
pages 126–27
Lejeune, 1977:131, 144
page 127, line 10
Brenner, 1978:30–31
page 128, line 22
Reiman, 1979:140
page 128, line 24
Rose, 1979:7
page 128, line 27
Williams, 1979:242
page 128, line 29
New York *Times*, News of the Week
in Review, Dec. 30, 1979
page 129, line 7
Liebow, 1967:50–52
page 130, line 10
Hill, 1980:47

page 130, line 35
Gutman, 1976
page 131, line 21
Spindler, 1979:81
page 131, line 24
Trader, 1979:549
page 131, line 32
Salamon, 1979:87
page 133, line 16
Stack, 1974
page 134, line 29
Sharff, 1980
page 135, line 27
Rein and Rainwater, 1976
page 137, line 13
Hill, 1979:32
page 138, line 3
Goldfarb, 1980
page 138, line 15
Hill, 1979:7

Chapter 8. Why the Cults Are Coming

page 142, line 10
Roszak, 1975:30
page 142, line 36
Bromley and Shupe, 1979:92
page 143, line 24
Harris, 1974:1978
page 143, line 32
Pritchard, 1976:299
pages 143–45
Bellah, 1976:341, 338, 339
page 147, line 13
Conway and Siegelman, 1978:169
page 147, line 22
Stone, 1976:100–101
page 147, line 27
Wallis, 1977
page 148, line 29
Op. cit., 121
page 148, line 35
Op. cit., 238
page 149, line 3
Malko, 1970:84

page 149, line 24
Wood, 1979:86–87
page 150, line 14
Edwards, 1979:158
page 150, line 23
Underwood and Underwood,
1979:76
page 150, line 27
Welles, 1978:255
page 151, line 18
Kroeber, 1925:40
page 152, line 2
Wall Street Journal, Jan. 23,
1979
page 153, line 15
Rodseth, 1980:16
page 154, line 6
Nugent, 1979
page 155, line 31
Wooden, 1981
page 156, line 4
Feinsod, 1981
page 156, line 9
Nugent, 1979:215
page 159, line 9
Christianity Today, 1980:24(13), 54

page 160, line 14
Playboy, Oct. 1980:159
page 160, line 27
Singer, 1980
page 161, line 2
Fairlee, 1980:17
page 161, line 6
Time, Oct. 1, 1979:68
page 161, line 22
Newsweek, Sept. 10, 1979:79
page 162, line 25
Dabney, 1980
page 163, lines 10, 27
Rifkin, 1979:107–8
page 164, line 18
Op.cit., 45

Chapter 9. Why America Changed

page 175, line 9
Elgin and Mitchell, 1977
page 175, line 10
Rifkin, 1980:208
page 177, line 7
Gilder, 1981:256
page 177, line 31
Op. cit., 68

Bibliography

Adam, Barry. "A Social History of Gay Politics," *in* Martin B. Levine, ed., *Gay Men: The Sociology of Male Homosexuality*. New York: Harper/Colophon, 1979, pp. 285–300.

Altman, Dennis. *Homosexual Oppression and Liberation*. New York: Avon/Discus, 1973.

Andreasen, Alan and Arthur Bert. "Consumers Complain—Does Business Respond?" *Harvard Business Review* 55 (1977): 93–100.

Bacon, Robert and Walter Eltis. *Britain's Economic Problem: Too Few Producers*. London: Macmillan, 1978.

Bane, Mary Jo. *Here to Stay: American Families in the Twentieth Century*. New York: Basic Books, 1976.

Barnet, Richard J. and Ronald E. Müller. *Global Reach*. New York: Simon and Schuster, 1974.

Bell, Daniel. *The Coming of Post-Industrial Society: A Venture in Social Forecasting*. New York: Basic Books, 1973.

Bellah, Robert. "New Religious Consciousness and the Crisis in Modernity," *in* Robert Bellah and Charles Glock, eds., *The New Religious Consciousness*. Berkeley: University of California Press, 1979, pp. 297–330.

Bentham, Jeremy. "Offenses Against One's Self: Pederasty." *Journal of Homosexuality* 3 (1978): 389–405.

Bernard, Jessie. "The Family in the Future." Courses by Newspaper. University Extension, University of California, San Diego, 1980.

Binstock, S. L. "Northrup DSD Spreads the Word About Reliability." *Quality Progress,* February 1980, 28–30.

Blake, Judith and P. Das Gupta. "Reproductive Motivation Versus Contraceptive Technology: Is Recent American Experience an Exception?" *Population and Development Review* 1 (1975): 229–249.

Braverman, Harry. *Labor and Monopoly Capital: The Degradation of Work in the Twentieth Century.* New York: Monthly Review Press, 1975.

Brenner, Harvey M. Testimony: Hearings Before the Subcommittee on Crime, House of Representatives. Ninety-Fifth Congress, Serial No. 47. Washington, D.C.: U.S. Government Printing Office, 28–54. 1978.

Bromley, David and Anson Shupe. *Moonies in America: Cult, Church, and Crusade.* Beverly Hills: Sage, 1979.

Brown, Ronald. Testimony: Hearings Before the Subcommittee on Crime, House of Representatives. Ninety-Fifth Congress, Serial No. 47. Washington, D.C.: U.S. Government Printing Office. 1978.

Brownlee, W. Elliot. "Household Values, Women's Work, and Economic Growth 1800–1930." *Journal of Economic History,* 1979.

Bullough, Vern. *Sex, Society and History.* New York: Science History Publication, 1976.

Butz, William and Michael Ward. "Baby Boom and Baby Bust: A New View," *American Demographics Magazine,* 1979.

Carter, Rose and Lois Dilatush. " 'Office Ladies' " *in* Joyce Lebra, Joy Paulson, and Elizabeth Powers, eds., *Women in Changing Japan.* Palo Alto: Stanford University Press, 1976, pp. 75–87.

Cohen, Stanley. "Discussion," *in Product Quality, Performance and Cost.* Washington, D.C.: National Academy of Engineering, 1972.

Conway, Flo and Jim Siegelman. *Snapping: America's Epidemic of Sudden Personality Change.* Philadelphia: Lippincott, 1978.

Conyers, John. "Unemployment Is Cruel and Unusual Punishment." *In* Hearings Before the Subcommittee on Crime, House of Representatives. Ninety-Fifth Congress, Serial No. 47. Washington, D.C.: U.S. Government Printing Office, 1978, pp. 674–679.

"Criminology, Economics, and Public Policy." *Crime and Delinquency* (1979) 25: 137–144.

Cudlipp, Edythe. *Understanding Women's Liberation*. New York: Paperback Library, 1971.

Dabney, Dick. "God's Own Network." *Harper's Magazine,* August 1980, pp. 33–52.

Degler, Carl. *At Odds: Women and the Family in America from the Revolution to the Present*. New York: Cambridge University Press, 1980.

Diamond, Stanley. "Anthropology in Question," *in* Dell Hymes, ed., *Reinventing Anthropology*. New York: Random House, 1972, pp. 401–429.

Doleschal, Eugene. "Sources of Basic Criminal Justice Statistics: A Brief Annotated Guide with Commentaries," *in Criminal Justice Abstracts,* March 1979, pp. 122–147.

———, and Anne Newton. "International Rates of Imprisonment." The National Council on Crime and Delinquency Information Center. Hackensack, N.J., 1979.

Dover, K. J. *Greek Homosexuality*. Cambridge: Harvard University Press, 1978.

Drummond, Isabel. *The Sex Paradox*. New York: G. P. Putnam, 1953.

Edwards, Christopher. *Crazy For God*. Englewood Cliffs, N.J.: Prentice-Hall, 1979.

Elgin, Duane and Arnold Mitchell. "Voluntary Simplicity: Life-Style of the Future?" *The Futurist* XI (1977): 200 ff.

Elshtain, Jean. "Feminists Against the Family." *The Nation,* November 17, 1979, 481ff.

Ennis, Philip. "Crime, Victims, and the Police," *in Modern Criminals*. New Brunswick: Transaction Books, pp. 89–117.

Epstein, Cynthia. *Woman's Place*. Berkeley: University of California Press, 1970.

Espenshade, Thomas J. *The Cost of Children in Urban United States*. Westport: Greenwood Press, 1977.

Evans, Joel, ed. *Consumerism in the United States: An Inter-Industry Analysis*. New York: Praeger, 1980, pp. 11–46.

Evans-Pritchard, E. E. "Sexual Inversion Among the Azande." *American Anthropologist* 72 (1970): 1428–1434.

Fairlee, Henry. "Born Again Bland." *New Republic,* August 2 and 9, 1980, pp. 16–20.

Federal Bureau of Investigation. *Uniform Crime Report*. Washington, D.C.: U.S. Government Printing Office, 1980.

Feinsod, Ethan. *Awake in a Nightmare*. New York: Norton, 1981.

Feyerabend, Paul. "Problems of Empiricism, Part II," *in* R. Colodny, ed., *Nature and Function of Scientific Theories*. Pittsburgh: University of Pittsburgh Press, 1970, pp. 275–353.

Fishman, Mark. "Crime Wave As Ideology." *Social Problems* 25 (1978): 531–543.

Ford, C. S. and F. A. Beach. *Patterns of Sexual Behavior.* New York: Harper and Row, 1970.

Friedan, Betty. "Feminism Takes a New Turn." *New York Times Magazine,* November 18, 1979, pp. 40ff.

Galbraith, John K. *Almost Everyone's Guide to Economics.* Boston: Houghton Mifflin, 1978.

Glenn, Evelyn and Roslyn Feldberg. "Degraded and Deskilled: The Proletarianization of Clerical Work," *in Social Problems* 25 (October) 1977: 52–64.

Goldfarb, Robert. *New York Times* "Op. Ed." page, March 14, 1980.

Gordon, Robert. *Economic Instability and Growth: The American Record.* New York: Harper and Row, 1974.

Griffith, Liddon. *Mugging: You Can Protect Yourself.* Englewood Cliffs, N.J.: Prentice-Hall, 1978.

Gutman, Herbert. *The Black Family in Slavery and Freedom.* New York: Pantheon Books, 1976.

Hacker, Helen. "A Functional Approach to the Gainful Employment of Married Women." Ph.D. Dissertation, Columbia University, 1961.

Harrington, Michael. *Decade of Decision.* New York: Simon and Schuster, 1980.

Harris, Marvin. *Cows, Pigs, Wars and Witches: The Riddles of Culture.* New York: Random House, 1974.

———. *Cannibals and Kings. The Origins of Cultures.* New York: Vintage, 1978.

Heilbroner, Robert and Lester Thurow. *Five Economic Challenges.* Englewood Cliffs, N.J.: Prentice-Hall, 1981.

Hill, Robert. "The Economic Status of Black Families," *in The State of Black America.* National Urban League, 1979, pp. 25–40. "Black Families in the 1970's" *in The State of Black America.* National Urban League, 1980, pp. 29–58.

Hindelang, Michael. "Race and Involvement in Common Law Personal Crimes." *American Sociological Review* 43 (1978): 93–109.

Hite, Shere. *The Hite Report: A Nationwide Study of Female Sexuality.* New York: Macmillan, 1976.

Howe, Louise Kapp. *Pink Collar Workers.* New York: Avon, 1977.

Job, Barbara Cottman. "Employment and Pay Trends in the Retail Trade Industry." *Monthly Labor Review,* March 1980, pp. 40–43.

Joint Economic Committee. *Report of the Joint Economic Committee.* Washington, D.C.: U.S. Government Printing Office, 1980.

Juran, J. M. "Quality and Income," *in* J. M. Juran, F. Gryna and R. S. Bingham Jr., eds., *Quality Control Handbook*. New York: McGraw-Hill, 1974, 3rd edition, 4.1–4.37. "Japanese and Western Quality: A Contrast," *in Quality Progress,* December 1978, pp. 10–18.

Kelly, Raymond. "Witchcraft and Sexual Relations" *in* P. Brown and G. Buchbinder, eds., *Man and Woman in the New Guinea Highlands*. American Anthropological Association, Special Publication 8 (1976): pp. 36–53.

Kolko, Gabriel. "The Structure of the Working Class and the Working Wife," *in* I. L. Horowitz et al., eds., *The American Working Class: Prospects for the 1980's*. New Brunswick, N.J.: Transaction Books, 1979, pp. 95–113.

Kroeber, Alfred. *The Yurok. Handbook of the Indians of California*. Bureau of American Ethnology, Bulletin 78, 1925.

Lasko, Keith. *The Great Billion Dollar Medical Swindle*. New York: Bobbs-Merrill, 1980.

Lee, John. "The Gay Connection." *Urban Life* 8 (1979): 175–198.

Lejeune, Robert. "The Management of a Mugging." *Urban Life* 6 (1977): 123–148.

Lekachman, Robert. "The Crash of 1980." *The Nation,* July 5, 1980.

Lester, Marianne. "Projects, Politics, Power: The Heart of the Controversy," *in* I. L. Horowitz, ed., *Science, Sin and Scholarship*. Cambridge: MIT Press, 1978, pp. 149–159.

Levine, Martin, "Gay Ghetto," *in* Martin Levine, ed., *Gay Men: The Sociology of Male Homosexuality*. New York: Harper/Colophon, 1979, pp. 182–204.

Liebow, Elliot. *Tally's Corner: A Study of Negro Street-Corner Men*. Boston: Little-Brown, 1967.

Lipsky, Michael. *Street-Level Bureaucracy: Dilemmas of the Individual in Public Services*. New York: Russell Sage Foundation, 1980.

Magdoff, Harry and Paul Sweezy. *The End of Prosperity*. New York: Monthly Review Press, 1977.

Malko, George. *Scientology: The Now Religion*. New York: Delta (Dell), 1970.

Margolis, Maxine. "From Betsy Ross Through Rosie the Riveter: Changing Attitudes Towards Women in the Labor Force." *Michigan Discussions in Anthropology* 3 (1977): 1–40.

Melman, Seymour. *The Permanent War Economy*. New York: Simon and Schuster, 1974.

Messer, Jeanne. "Guru Maharaj Ji and the Divine Light Mission," *in* Robert Bellah and Charles Glock, eds., *The New Religious Con-*

sciousness. Berkeley: University of California Press, 1976, pp. 52–72.

Mills, Jeannie. *Six Years with God: Life Inside Reverend Jim Jones' Peoples Temple*. New York: A & W Publishers, 1979.

Minge, Wanda. *The Rise of the Cost of Children: Family Economics in Historical Perspective*. Chicago: University of Chicago Press (in press).

Minge-Kalman, Wanda. "The Industrial Revolution and the European Family: The Institutionalization of 'Childhood' as a Market for Family Labor." *Comparative Studies in Society and History* 20 (1978): 454–468.

Mulvihill, D., M. Tumin, and L. Curtis. *A Staff Report Submitted to the National Commission on the Causes and Prevention of Violence. Crimes of Violence* Vol. II, Washington, D.C.: U.S. Government Printing Office, 1969.

National Criminal Justice Information and Statistics Service. Criminal Victimization in the United States. SD-NCS N-9-NCJ-49543. Washington, D.C.: U.S. Government Printing Office, 1976.

Nugent, John. *White Night*. New York: Rawson, Wade, 1979.

Nussbaum, Karen. *Race Against Time*. Cleveland: National Association of Office Workers, 1980.

Okun, Arthur. "The Balanced Budget is a Placebo." *Challenge*, May–June 1980, p. 3.

Papanek, Victor and James Hennessey. *How Things Don't Work*. New York: Pantheon Books, 1977.

Pascale, Richard and Anthony Athos. *The Art of Japanese Management*. New York: Simon and Schuster, 1981.

Pifer, Alan. "Perceptions of Childhood and Youth." Reprinted from the 1978 Annual Report of the Carnegie Corporation of New York.

Ploscowe, Morris. *Sex and Law*. New York: Prentice-Hall, 1951.

Porat, Marc. "The Information Economy." Ph.D. Dissertation, Stanford University, 1976.

Pritchard, Linda. "Religious Change in Nineteenth Century America," *in* Robert Bellah and Charles Glock, eds., *The New Religious Consciousness*. Berkeley: University of California Press, 1976, pp. 297–330.

Raphael, Edna. "Working Women and Their Membership in Labor Unions," *in* I. L. Horowitz et al., eds., *The American Working Class: Prospects for the 1980's*. New Brunswick, N.J.: Transaction Books, 1979, pp. 95–113.

Reiman, Jeffry. *The Rich Get Richer and the Poor Get Prison: Class and Criminal Justice*. New York: John Wiley, 1979.

Rein, Martin and Lee Rainwater. "How Large Is the Welfare Class," *in Change,* September–October 1977, pp. 20–23.

Rifkin, Jeremy. *Entropy: A New World View.* New York: Viking, 1980.

———, and Ted Howard. *The Emerging Order: God in the Age of Scarcity.* New York: Putnam, 1979.

Ringer, Robert. *Restoring the American Dream.* New York: Harper and Row, 1979.

Rodseth, Bob. "Pyramid Players: Exponents of the Exponent." *The Gambling Scene,* June 1980, pp. 14–16.

Rollin, Betty. "Motherhood: Who Needs It?" *in* Louise Kapp Howe, ed., *The Future of the Family.* New York: Touchstone/Simon and Schuster, 1977, pp. 69–82.

Rose, Harold M. "Lethal Aspects of Urban Violence: An Overview," *in* Harold Rose, ed., *Lethal Aspects of Urban Violence.* Lexington, Mass.: Lexington Books, 1979, pp. 1–16.

Ross, Ruth and G. Benson. "Criminal Justice from East to West." *Crime and Delinquency 25* (1979): 76–86.

Roszak, Theodore. *Unfinished Animal: The Aquarian Frontier and the Evolution of Consciousness.* New York: Harper and Row, 1975.

Ryscavage, Paul. "More Wives in Labor Force Have Husbands with Above Average Incomes." *Monthly Labor Review 102* (1979): 40–42.

Salamon, Lester. *Welfare: The Elusive Consensus.* New York: Praeger, 1978.

Seward, Rudy R. *The American Family: A Demographic History.* Beverly Hills: Sage, 1978.

Sharff, Jagna. "Life on Dolittle Street: How Poor People Purchase Immortality." Ms. Hispanic Study Project. Columbia University, 1980.

Shorter, Edward. *The Making of the American Family.* New York: Basic Books, 1975.

Silverman, David. *Reading Castaneda: A Prologue to the Social Sciences.* London: Routledge and Kegan Paul, 1975.

Singer, Benjamin. "Incommunicado Social Machines." *Social Policy,* 1979.

Singer, David. "The Crystal Cathedral: Reflections of Schuller's Theology." *Christianity Today,* August 8, 1980, pp. 28–29.

Skogan, Wesley. "Crime in Contemporary America," *in* H.D. Graham and T.R. Gurr, eds., *Violence in America: Historical and Comparative Perspective.* Beverly Hills: Sage, 1979, pp. 375–391.

Slater, Courtenay and T. Kraseman. "Work Styles in Services, Trade Changes to Accommodate Needs of New Worker." *Business America*, April 23, 1979, pp. 18–19.

Smith, Ralph. "The Movement of Women into the Labor Force," *in* Ralph Smith, ed., *The Subtle Revolution*. Washington, D.C.: The Urban Institute, 1979.

Smith-Rosenberg, Carroll. "Sex as Symbol in Victorian Purity: An Ethnohistorical Analysis of Jacksonian America," *in* J. Demos and S. S. Boocock, eds., *Turning Points*. Supplement to the *American Journal of Sociology* 84.

Spindler, Arthur. *Public Welfare*. New York: Human Sciences Press, 1979.

Stack, Carol. *All Our Kin: Strategies for Survival in a Black Community*. New York: Harper and Row, 1974.

Stanback, Thomas. *Understanding the Service Economy: Employment, Productivity, Location*. Baltimore: Johns Hopkins Press, 1979.

Sterling, T. D. "Consumer Difficulties with Computerized Transactions: An Empirical Investigation." *Communications of the ACM* 22 (1979): 283–289.

Stone, Donald. "The Human Potential Movement," *in* Robert Bellah and Charles Glock, eds., *The New Religious Consciousness*. Berkeley: University of California Press, 1976, pp. 93–115.

Sukenick, Ronald. "Upward and Juanward: The Possible Dream," *in* Daniel Noel, ed., *Seeing Castaneda: Reactions to the "Don Juan" Writings of Carlos Castaneda*. New York: Putnam, 1976, pp. 110–120.

Taylor, Gordon Rattray. *Sex in History*. New York: Vanguard Press, 1954.

Thurow, Lester. *The Zero-Sum Society*. New York: Basic Books, 1980.

Toffler, Alvin. *The Third Wave*. New York: William Morrow, 1980.

Trader, Harriet. "Welfare Policies and Black Families." *Social Work* (1979) 24: 548–552.

Turchi, Boone. *The Demand for Children: The Economics of Fertility in the United States*. Cambridge, Mass.: Ballinger, 1975.

Underwood, Barbara and Betty Underwood. *Hostage to Heaven*. New York: Clarkson W. Potter, 1979.

Ungaretti, John. "Pederasty, Heroism, and the Family in Classical Greece." *Journal of Homosexuality* 3 (1978): 291–300.

UNESCO. *The Determinants and Consequences of Population Trends*. New York: ST/SOA/SER.A/50, 1973.

United States Bureau of Census. *Historical Statistics of the United*

States: Colonial Times to 1970. Washington, D.C.: U.S. Government Printing Office, 1975.

United States National Criminal Justice Information and Statistics Service. *Myths and Realities About Crime*. Washington, D.C.: U.S. Government Printing Office, 1978.

United States Statistical Abstract. Washington, D.C.: U.S. Government Printing Office, 1980.

Vogel, Ezra. *Japan As Number One: Lessons for America*. Cambridge: Harvard University Press, 1979.

Wallis, Roy. *The Road to Total Freedom: A Sociological Analysis of Scientology*. New York: Columbia University Press, 1977.

Wattenberg, Esther and Hazel Reinhardt. "Female-Headed Families: Trends and Implications." *Social Work,* November 1979, pp. 460–467.

Welles, Chris. "The Eclipse of Sun Myung Moon," *in* Irving Horowitz, ed., *Science, Sin and Scholarship*. Cambridge: MIT Press, 1978, pp. 243–258.

Westoff, Charles. "Marriage and Fertility in the Developed Countries." *Scientific American* 239 (December 1978): 51ff.

Williams, James, ed. *The State of Black America*. New York: National Urban League, 1979.

Wittman, Carl. "A Gay Manifesto," *in* Karla Jay and Allen Young, eds., *Out of the Closets*. New York: Jove (Harcourt Brace Jovanovich), 1970, pp. 330–342.

Wolf, Deborah, *The Lesbian Community*. Berkeley: University of California Press, 1979.

Wood, Allen and Jack Vitek. *Moonstruck: A Memoir of My Life in a Cult*. New York: William Morrow, 1979.

Wooden, Kenneth. *The Children of Jonestown*. New York: McGraw-Hill, 1981.

Wright, J. Patrick. *On a Clear Day You Can See General Motors*. Grosse Pointe, Mich.: Wright Enterprises, 1979.

Index